This book is from

the kitchen library of

_____

_____

ALSO BY ART GINSBURG, MR. FOOD®

The Mr. Food® Cookbook, OOH IT'S SO GOOD!!™ (1990)

Mr. Food® Cooks Like Mama (1992)

Mr. Food® Cooks Chicken (1993)

Mr. Food® Cooks Pasta (1993)

Mr. Food® Makes Dessert (1993)

Mr. Food® Cooks Real American (1994)

Mr. Food®'s Favorite Cookies (1994)

Mr. Food®'s Quick and Easy Side Dishes (1995)

Mr. Food® Grills It All in a Snap (1995)

Mr. Food®'s Fun Kitchen Tips and Shortcuts (and Recipes, Too!) (1995)

Mr. Food®'s Old World Cooking Made Easy (1995)

"Help, Mr. Food®! Company's Coming!" (1995)

Mr. Food® Pizza 1-2-3 (1996)

Mr. Food® Meat Around the Table (1996)

Mr. Food® Simply Chocolate (1996)

Mr. Food® A Little Lighter (1996)

Mr. Food® From My Kitchen to Yours: Stories and Recipes from Home (1996)

Mr. Food® Easy Tex-Mex (1997)

Mr. Food® One Pot, One Meal (1997)

Mr. Food® Cool Cravings (1997)

Mr. Food®'s Italian Kitchen (1997)

Mr. Food's

Simple Southern Favorites

Art Ginsburg
Mr. Food®

WILLIAM MORROW AND COMPANY, INC.

NEW YORK

Library of Congress Cataloging-in-Publication Data

Ginsburg, Art.
    Mr. Food®'s simple southern favorites / Art Ginsburg.
        p.   cm.
    ISBN 0-688-14580-9
    1. Cookery, American—Southern style.   2. Quick and easy cookery.
I. Title.
TX715.2.S68G55   1997   97-28594
641.5975—dc21   CIP

Printed in the United States of America

First Edition

1   2   3   4   5   6   7   8   9   10

BOOK DESIGN BY MICHAEL MENDELSOHN OF MM DESIGN 2000, INC.

www.williammorrow.com

www.mrfood.com

DEDICATED TO

The South —
Where sitting down to a meal has always meant
sharing comfort, warmth, and family.

WITH SPECIAL THANKS TO MY FRIEND

Sema Wilkes of Mrs. Wilkes' Boarding House in
Savannah, Georgia
Where the feelings of true Southern hospitality
are still being shared . . . and preserved.

"OOH IT'S SO GOOD!!®"

$\mathcal{A}$cknowledgments

Throughout this book we talk about hospitality. That means opening our kitchens, actually our homes, and sharing whatever we have. And during the months of creating and testing these recipes, I was lucky to be surrounded by people who opened up and shared their stories and tastes of the South so that I could come up with quick and easy recipes to share with you.

This book wouldn't have been possible without the unbelievable staff I work side by side with in our test kitchen. Janice Bruce, a true Southern belle, was instrumental in providing the Southern authenticity and helping shape it into the Mr. Food style. Patty Rosenthal, Cheryl Gerber, and Joan Wolff, my kitchen "dream team," now all have a bit of the South in them! Boy, did we cook up batch after batch of Southern hospitality! Joe Peppi not only was an integral part of the overall layout of the book, but he checked and rechecked us for accuracy every step of the way. A big welcome to "Charlie" Tallant, who joined our team to input all the recipes into the computer, and a big thank-you to our all-around kitchen helper, Al Barron.

Along the way I could even relax occasionally with an ice-cold lemonade, knowing that Caryl Ginsburg Fantel and Howard Rosenthal were overseeing every aspect of the book's production. Thanks again, guys!

I also thank Helayne Rosenblum for her expert research and for tweaking my ideas. I truly appreciate the support I get each and every day from the rest of my team—my wife, Ethel, who's always there for me *and* who skillfully helps me answer all my viewer and reader mail; my sons, Steve Ginsburg, who oversees the Mr. Food operation, and Chuck Ginsburg, who keeps everything running smoothly for our 150-plus TV stations; Tom Palombo, our licensing agent, who always seems to keep me going in new and interesting directions; and Chet Rosenbaum, our controller, who keeps us all in line so masterfully. Of course, you'll find some real Southern hospitality from the rest of my support staff, too. These are the folks who really keep everything humming for the whole team: Carol Ginsburg, Marilyn Ruderman, Alice Palombo, Heidi Triveri, and Beth Ives.

Oh, let's not forget to mention Bill Wright, President and CEO of the Hearst Book Group, and all the folks at William Morrow, including Paul Fedorko, Publisher and Senior Vice President; Editor Zachary Schisgal; and Assistant Editor Anne Cole. And yes, there's more: Richard Aquan, Deborah Weiss Geline, Lisa Dolin, Michael Murphy, and Jackie Deval. And when it comes to the final touches, designer Michael Mendelsohn and illustrator Philip Scheuer bring it all together like no one else.

And, of course, there's Bill Adler, my agent, who gets the ball rolling and keeps it going!

When it really comes down to hospitality and opening our homes, I have to thank all of my viewers and readers who always share so much with me—from family recipes to warm wishes and thoughts. You really mean so much to me!

Last but not least, I thank all the food councils and companies that consistently make themselves and their information available to me. That's just what Southern hospitality is all about.

Contents

Introduction

A number of years ago, when I was visiting WTOC-TV, my station in Savannah, Georgia (what a city!), I stopped by Mrs. Wilkes' Boarding House, a small down-home eating establishment with a big reputation. As I walked into Mrs. Wilkes' simple dining room, I felt something. No, it wasn't my stomach rumbling! It was a warm feeling all over. I felt as if I'd just walked into the home of an old friend.

As I enjoyed my scrumptious meal at a table along with other guests (it's family style all the way there!), it hit me! What made this place so darned special was the Southern hospitality. It wasn't fancy—it was just a good time with good people and heaps of fabulous, casual food. And with each forkful, I became more and more determined that someday I'd get to share this feeling and the tastes of the South in one of my own books.

So here it is! I'm sharing my Simple Southern Favorites with you. Now you may be wondering what areas I'm talking about when I talk about the South. Well, as I got into the research for this book I found out that everybody's got a different idea of just what areas are considered "the South." So I've included stories and foods from a wide area . . . and I'm sure you'll find what you're looking for!

The South is really quite a diverse area. What makes it so, other than its geographical location? It's the agriculture, the climate, the food, and, most of all, the people. With my recipes and stories I've tried to re-create that incredible feeling that I first experienced in Savannah. So please join me on my mouthwatering tour of the South!

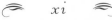

Like a warm welcome, the aroma of Southern cooking wraps around you almost immediately after you walk into a home or restaurant. As I recall from my visits to Mrs. Wilkes' it's the tantalizing smell of breads and biscuits baking (and the incredible tastes that are even better than the aromas!) that gets your taste buds ready for true Southern food experiences.

So that's why we start off with a chapter of all kinds of easy breads and biscuits, from Old-fashioned Buttermilk Biscuits and Refrigerator Spoon Rolls to a simple classic Sally Lunn Bread and, of course, Peanut Butter Muffins. Each of them is special.

Now, in the South you can always count on tasty pickles, relishes, jams, jellies, and other nibbles to enjoy along with fresh-from-the-oven goodies. Maybe you'd like to spread a little Blue Ribbon Strawberry Preserves or Pepper Jelly on an Angel Flake Biscuit, then crunch away on Plantation Pickle Chips. Or maybe you'll decide to relish the moment with Sweet Pepper Relish or Carolina Marinated Mushrooms.

When you're good and ready to dig in, the Southern soup pot offers so many tasty options. Should it be Butter Bean and Ham Soup, Tomato-Crab Bisque, or maybe a big bowl of Brunswick Stew? Whichever you choose, you'll find lots of tasty soup and stew recipes to simmer in your soup pot.

And when the mercury rises and you're looking for a summer salad to crunch on, wait till you see what I've got for you! Make-Ahead Refrigerator Salad is my first choice 'cause it's so colorful, but I've got a load of other great choices, including Curried Chicken Salad, Vinegar Slaw, and Sweet Relish–Potato Salad. Of course there's Plantation Fruit Salad, Strawberry Patch Salad, Pineapple-Carrot Salad, and other cool and refreshing fruit salads, too.

Now, for that porch luncheon or reception, you're gonna be interested in what I call my party platter foods—spreads, sandwiches, and other easy-to-eat munchies like Cheesy Corn Roll-ups, Cola Meatballs, Snackin' Pecans, and a Pimiento Cheese Ball that practically makes its own party when served up with Cheese Straws or Nutty Cheese Crackers.

A tour of the South wouldn't be complete without barbecue! And I've got lots of choices for you here. Now, when Southerners talk about barbecue, they're not referring to food simply cooked on a grill and slathered with thick barbecue sauce. It's more a *way* of cooking—over a pit of glowing coals for a long time. And each region seems to have its own special barbecue flavors, as you'll see from the variety of flavorings in these dishes and the sauces I've included. But since I don't expect you to dig a pit in your backyard to make authentic barbecue, I've adjusted my recipes so they can be made right in the oven or broiler, or on the stove.

Southerners are so serious about their barbecue . . . it's practically a way of life! So you've gotta try easy-as-can-be Stovetop Barbecued Roast and Smothered Pork Chops. Or if chicken is your preference, go for the Peach-Glazed Chicken or the Sweet Mustard Barbecued Chicken. Or mix and match your favorite meats and poultry with any of the flavor-packed barbecue sauces here.

All right, our tempting tour of the South is now ready for a stop at the meat case. Wait till you dig into main-dish meats like Bourbon Steaks from Tennessee or Southern-Fried Pork Chops so moist they're sure to become a family favorite. With more than twenty-five selections of pork, beef, and lamb, you'll never get bored!

If you're a chicken fan, boy, are you in luck! Of course I've got The One and Only Fried Chicken. Then there are other down-home favorites such as Chicken with Peanuts, Mustard-Pecan Chicken Fillets, Tangy Buttermilk Chicken, and so many more!

We can't forget about all the fresh seafood found off the

Southern coasts. Oysters are certainly no stranger to Southern tables. And we've got 'em made lots of different ways. Mouthwatering Crab Cakes are definitely one of my favorites. So is Perfect Fried Shrimp!

Maybe freshwater fish is more to your liking—it sure is mild and sweet. So try Fried Catfish or Trout Fish-Fry. Yup, whether it's fried, boiled, scalloped, or sautéed, Southern seafood's sure a treat!

Now, let's talk about what goes with all these scrumptious main dishes. You know, you won't find a Southern meal served without a selection of garden-fresh veggies. Butter-Glazed Carrots, Cheesy Cauliflower, and Home-style Corn Pudding are a good way to ease yourself in. But then you're gonna want to dig deep down to our Southern roots and dish up some Steamin' Collards or Fried Okra. One of my traditional favorites that's really easy to make is Fried Green Tomatoes, but every one of these dishes says, "Welcome to dinner!"

Mmm, mmm! Crunchy outside and soft inside, Hush Puppies are so easy to pop in your mouth. Know how they got their name? Check out the recipe and find out! Other popular hearty go-alongs that just can't be missed are Shredded Sweet Potatoes, Sage Corn Bread Dressing, and True Fried Grits. You can't get more Southern than that!

Even when our bellies are full, we *must* accept dessert. After all, we have to be polite guests—and, anyway, it's almost impossible to turn away an offering from the cake shop! Layers of Watermelon Cake (yes, made with fresh watermelon) and Old-fashioned Southern Chocolate Cake will make you want to become a permanent Southern resident. Then there's Easy Peach Cake and Bourbon Fruitcake that go together in no time at all. There are loads of icings to go along with these yummy cakes, too, to make them truly irresistible!

The dessert section wouldn't be complete without sweet

Southern treats—pies from Polka Dot Peach to Lemon Chess and fresh strawberry (it tastes as if it was just picked!). And the choices don't stop there. With all the cobblers, custards, puddings, parfaits, fritters, pralines, and fudge, we may want to skip dinner and go straight to dessert!

But we can't finish until we wash it all down, so let's head for my last chapter and stir up some icy Country Lemonade, Hot Spiced Cider, punches and more punches, and, of course, a Mint Julep (for adults only) on Derby day, or any day.

Well, now you've got a choice—to enjoy the tastes and warmth of true Southern hospitality, you can either head South on the Interstate or open up to a recipe or two or three . . . which means you're in for a load of

"OOH IT'S SO GOOD!!®"

"Southern Light"

Tips for Lightening Up Southern Favorites

Traditional Southern cooking can be thought of as heavy and rich—with much frying done in fatback, and many dishes using extra-creamy butter, lots of cheese, and the richest cream. Those touches sure do add flavor and texture to dishes, but with moderation so much a part of our lives today, we can cut down a little here and there to reduce fat, calories, cholesterol, sodium, and sugar where we need to.

I've already cut back somewhat in many of these recipes, but you and your doctor are the ones who know what's best for you. And to help you moderate these recipes even more, here are a few easy substitutions and tips that'll help you cook and eat more moderately without sacrificing flavor:

- Canned soups are a great beginning for sauces and casseroles. If we choose lighter or reduced-fat or reduced-sodium versions, we can sure save calories and cut down on fat and sodium.

- Select oils such as canola or safflower for frying; they're lower in saturated fat than other types.

- When frying, make sure you heat your oil until hot but not smoking. Simply using the right-temperature oil will help reduce the fat that's absorbed into food when it cooks. Frying oil should stay *outside* your food!

- Drain all fried foods on clean paper towels to remove as much excess oil as possible.

- When a recipe calls for peanuts, pecans, or other nuts, don't be afraid to cut down the amount. Usually we can cut the amount in half and still get great flavor and texture.

- In many cases, we can replace whole eggs with egg whites. (Two egg whites equal one whole egg.) And, yes, in most recipes, you can go ahead and replace eggs altogether with egg substitute. (It's usually available near the eggs in the refrigerated section of the supermarket). However, I don't recommend using egg substitute when coating foods for breading. Breading doesn't stick to it very well.

- Choose lean cuts of meat and trim away any visible fat before preparing. Serve moderate-sized portions, like 3 to 4 ounces of cooked meat (about 4 to 6 ounces raw) per adult. (That's about the size of a deck of playing cards.) And with ground meats, select leaner blends, preferably ones that have a 90/10 meat-to-fat ratio. (Traditional ground beef and pork usually have a 70/30 ratio.)

- Choose cooking methods (like roasting, broiling, grilling, and baking on a rack) that allow fat to drip away during cooking.

- In most recipes, you can replace ground beef or pork with turkey. Keep in mind, though, that ground turkey needs more seasoning than beef and pork.

- If browning ground beef, pork, or turkey before adding it to a recipe, after browning, place it in a strainer, rinse it with warm water, then drain and continue as directed. This should remove most of the excess fat.

- In most recipes, you can replace whole chicken or parts with boneless and skinless chicken breasts. Remember that boneless breasts are generally thinner, so they'll cook more quickly than bone-in parts; adjust your cooking times accordingly.

- Remove the layer of fat that rises to the top of soups, stews, and pan juices of roasts. Chilling makes this a breeze, so it's even easier to do with dishes that are made ahead and chilled before being reheated. Or, a timesaving tip for removing fat from soups and stews is simply to add a few ice cubes to a warm cooked dish. As soon as the fat sticks to the cubes, remove them, and the fat will come out right along with them!

- Let's look to our supermarket dairy case for some reduced-fat, low-fat, or fat-free alternatives. For instance, there's low-fat milk for our soups and sauces, instead of heavy cream. (Evaporated skim milk will work, too.) The same goes for our cheese choices. Experiment with those, or maybe just use a little less of the regular full-fat versions.

- When it comes to mayonnaise, there are lighter varieties available, too. And when using it in a salad, mix it in just before serving . . . you can usually get by with using less that way. Or sometimes I use a combination of half mayonnaise and half low-fat yogurt. It does the trick, too!

- Many desserts call for whipped cream or whipped topping. To watch calories and fat with those, we've got great choices available with reduced-fat and nonfat whipped toppings. You may need to increase the flavoring or sugar a bit, though, depending on the recipe.

If you're trying to cut down your fat, calorie, cholesterol, sodium, or sugar intake, the best advice is still to eat less overall. Of course, each of us has our own dietary requirements, so always consult your physician for your own specific guidelines. Then go ahead and make changes that'll work for you. That way, you'll be able to enjoy the "OOH IT'S SO GOOD!!®" for many years to come!

A Note About Packaged Foods

Packaged food sizes may vary by brand. Generally, the sizes indicated in these recipes are average sizes. If you can't find the exact package size listed in the ingredients, whatever package is closest in size will usually do the trick.

The Bread Basket

Biscuits, Rolls, Muffins, and Breads

Old-fashioned Buttermilk Biscuits

about 2 dozen

Incredibly light and fluffy, these'll melt in your mouth, just like Grandma's biscuits always did!

4 cups self-rising flour
1 tablespoon baking powder
1 tablespoon sugar

¾ cup vegetable shortening
2 cups buttermilk

Preheat the oven to 400°F. In a large bowl, combine the flour, baking powder, and sugar; mix well. Using a fork or pastry cutter, cut the shortening into the flour mixture until crumbly. Add the buttermilk and stir just until a soft dough forms. Lightly flour a work surface and use a rolling pin to roll out the dough 1 inch thick. Using a 3-inch biscuit or round cookie cutter, cut into biscuits and place on a large baking sheet that has been coated with nonstick cooking spray. Bake for 10 to 12 minutes, or until light golden. Serve warm, or remove to a wire rack to cool completely.

Note: Serve these with a little butter for the perfect addition to breakfast . . . or any meal, for that matter!

Soda Biscuits

about 1 dozen

What would Southern cooking be without biscuits? Did you know that these are called soda biscuits 'cause the baking soda is what makes 'em so Southern-special?

2½ cups all-purpose flour, divided
1 teaspoon baking soda
½ teaspoon baking powder
½ teaspoon salt
2 tablespoons vegetable shortening
1 cup buttermilk

Preheat the oven to 450°F. In a large bowl, combine 2 cups flour, the baking soda, baking powder, and salt; mix well. Using a fork or pastry cutter, cut the shortening into the flour mixture until crumbly. Add the buttermilk and stir just until blended. Spread the remaining ½ cup flour on a work surface and gently knead the dough with your hands, working in the ½ cup flour. Do not overwork the dough. Using a rolling pin, roll the dough out to a ½-inch thickness. With a 3-inch biscuit or round cookie cutter, cut the dough into biscuits. Place on a large baking sheet that has been coated with nonstick cooking spray and bake for 15 to 18 minutes, or until light golden. Serve warm, or remove to a wire rack to cool completely.

Note: I like to keep a container of powdered buttermilk on hand in my pantry. All I need to do is add water to the powder whenever I have a recipe that calls for buttermilk.

Angel Flake Biscuits

about 2½ dozen

If you're looking for a biscuit that's very flaky, look no more! With the yeast and the self-rising flour to fluff these up, you're in for a real treat!

¼ cup warm water
1 package (0.25 ounce) yeast
5½ cups self-rising flour, plus more for rolling out

¼ cup sugar
¾ cup vegetable shortening
2 cups buttermilk

Preheat the oven to 425°F. In a small bowl, combine the water and yeast and let stand for 5 minutes. In a large bowl, combine the flour and sugar. Using a fork or pastry cutter, cut the shortening into the flour mixture until crumbly. Add the yeast mixture and the buttermilk and stir until a soft dough forms. Generously flour a work surface and, with a floured rolling pin, roll out the dough ¾ inch thick. The dough will be sticky. With a 2½-inch biscuit cutter, cut the dough into biscuits and place on baking sheets that have been coated with nonstick cooking spray. Bake for 12 to 15 minutes, or until light golden. Serve immediately, or remove to a wire rack to cool completely.

Note: If you don't have a biscuit cutter, an appropriately sized drinking glass can be used to cut the biscuit rounds. If you don't want to make all the biscuits at once, the dough will keep in the refrigerator for several days. When ready to use, roll it out, cut it, and let it stand for 15 minutes before baking as directed.

Cheese Biscuits

about 2 dozen

Serve these up for breakfast, lunch, even dinner. I mean, how can we go wrong when we combine Cheddar cheese with our favorite biscuit dough?

2 cups self-rising flour, plus
   more for rolling out
1/2 cup (2 ounces) shredded
   sharp Cheddar cheese

2 tablespoons sugar
1/4 teaspoon cayenne pepper
½ cup vegetable shortening
⅔ cup buttermilk

Preheat the oven to 425°F. In a large bowl, combine the flour, cheese, sugar, and cayenne pepper; mix well. Using a fork or pastry cutter, cut the shortening into the flour mixture until crumbly. Add the buttermilk and stir until a dough forms. Knead the dough on a lightly floured work surface until smooth. With a rolling pin, roll out the dough ¼ inch thick. With a 2-inch biscuit cutter, cut into biscuits. Place on baking sheets that have been coated with nonstick cooking spray and bake for 10 to 12 minutes, or until light golden. Remove to a wire rack to cool completely.

Note: I sometimes like to add a little more cayenne pepper to give these an extra-spicy kick.

Refrigerator Spoon Rolls

about 3 dozen

These are a real Southern favorite 'cause the dough can be made ahead and kept in the fridge for weeks. That makes it easy to bake up some fresh rolls anytime we get drop-ins!

2 cups lukewarm water
1 package (0.25 ounce) yeast
4½ cups self-rising flour
¼ cup sugar

¾ cup (1½ sticks) butter, melted
1 egg

Preheat the oven to 400°F. In a small bowl, combine the water and yeast and let stand for 5 minutes. In a large bowl, combine the remaining ingredients; mix well. Add the yeast mixture and whisk for several minutes, until the dough is smooth. Drop by tablespoonfuls 1 inch apart onto rimmed baking sheets that have been coated with nonstick cooking spray. Bake for 12 to 15 minutes, or until light golden.

Note: If you *do* make this dough to have on hand in the fridge, keep it tightly covered. Then, when you're ready to enjoy fresh rolls, just drop and bake the dough as directed.

Beer Rolls

1 dozen

When the gang butters you up to make these, don't tell them they're so easy that you have a barrel of fun baking them up!

4 cups biscuit baking mix   1 can (12 ounces) beer
¼ cup sugar

Preheat the oven to 425°F. In a large bowl, combine all the ingredients; mix well. Spoon equally into 12 muffin cups that have been coated with nonstick cooking spray. Bake for 15 to 18 minutes, or until golden. Serve warm, or allow to cool slightly, then remove to a wire rack to cool completely.

Note: It's so simple to make these and keep 'em handy in the freezer in a resealable plastic storage bag. Then you can just pop 'em in the microwave or toaster oven to warm before serving.

Easy Mayo Rolls

1 dozen

The mayonnaise takes the place of eggs and oil in these, making moist throw-together rolls in just minutes!

3 cups self-rising flour
1½ cups milk

⅓ cup mayonnaise

Preheat the oven to 425°F. In a medium-sized bowl, combine all the ingredients; mix well. Spoon equally into 12 muffin cups that have been coated with nonstick cooking spray. Bake for 12 to 15 minutes, or until golden. Serve warm, or allow to cool slightly, then remove to a wire rack to cool completely.

Note: It's easy to have fresh rolls in no time with just three ingredients. Most of us keep milk and mayonnaise on hand, but you've gotta be sure to have *self-rising* flour on hand, too, so you can make these anytime.

Quick Cinnamon Rolls

1 dozen

This variation on an old favorite can be made so quickly, it'll be a sweet surprise!

1 tablespoon butter, melted
1½ teaspoons vanilla extract
¼ cup sugar
1½ teaspoons ground
   cinnamon

1 package (8 ounces)
   refrigerated crescent rolls

Preheat the oven to 350°F. In a small bowl, combine the butter and vanilla; mix well and set aside. In another small bowl, combine the sugar and cinnamon; mix well and set aside. Unroll the crescent rolls and pinch the seams together to form one large rectangle. Brush the butter mixture evenly over the dough, then sprinkle with the sugar mixture. Roll up the dough jelly-roll style, starting from a long side. Cut into 12 equal slices. Place the slices cut side down ½ inch apart in a 9-inch cake pan that has been coated with nonstick cooking spray. Bake for 18 to 20 minutes, or until golden. Remove from the oven and invert onto a serving plate. Allow to cool slightly; serve warm.

Note: If you want to make these ahead of time, prepare the dough in the cake pan, cover it with plastic wrap, and refrigerate it until just before ready to bake and serve.

Molasses Muffins

2 dozen

I got this recipe years ago from one of my viewers. And since she was an experienced home cook from the Deep South, I knew I had to include it here.

2 cups whole wheat flour
1 cup all-purpose flour
½ cup firmly packed light
　brown sugar
2 teaspoons baking soda

1 teaspoon salt
2 cups buttermilk
½ cup molasses
½ cup raisins

Preheat the oven to 250°F. In a large bowl, combine both flours, the brown sugar, baking soda, and salt; mix well. Add the buttermilk, molasses, and raisins; mix well. Spoon equally into 24 muffin cups that have been coated with nonstick cooking spray. Bake for 35 to 40 minutes, or until a wooden toothpick inserted in the center comes out clean. Allow to cool slightly, then remove to a wire rack to cool completely.

Note: To make cleanup easier, go ahead and use paper muffin cup liners in the muffin tins.

Peanut Butter Muffins

1 dozen

Sure, we could make peanut butter muffins by doing it the long way and grinding the peanuts first. But why do that when we can start off with jarred peanut butter? Personally, I think it gives us moister muffins doing it the easy way!

1 cup peanut butter	2 tablespoons butter, melted
2 eggs	2 cups biscuit baking mix
1 cup milk	¼ cup sugar

Preheat the oven to 400°F. In a medium-sized bowl, with an electric beater on low speed, beat the peanut butter and eggs. Add the milk and butter and continue beating until well combined. Add the biscuit baking mix and sugar; stir until just moistened. Spoon equally into 12 muffin cups that have been coated with nonstick cooking spray. Bake for 15 to 18 minutes, or until golden and a wooden toothpick inserted in the center comes out clean. Serve warm, or allow to cool slightly, then remove to a wire rack to cool completely.

Note: I like to serve these warm with a little strawberry jelly for the flavor and fun of a PB&J sandwich.

Country Corn Bread

9 to 12 servings

Oh boy, do I love to slather these with creamy butter or drizzle them with honey! I've even made my own honey butter by simply combining the two for those times when I couldn't decide which topping to choose.

3 cups cornmeal	¼ cup vegetable oil
1 cup all-purpose flour	2 tablespoons sugar
2 cups milk	1 tablespoon baking powder
2 eggs	1¼ teaspoons salt

Preheat the oven to 450°F. In a large bowl, combine all the ingredients; mix well. Pour the batter into an 8-inch square baking dish that has been coated with nonstick cooking spray. Bake for 30 to 35 minutes, or until golden and a wooden toothpick inserted in the center comes out clean. Cut and serve warm, or allow to cool before serving.

Note: If you have a large cast-iron skillet and would like to make crispy corn bread, place ⅓ cup vegetable oil in the skillet and heat in the 450°F. oven until hot. Remove from the oven and pour the batter over the hot oil. Return the skillet to the oven and bake as above.

Sally Lunn Bread

This bread, "the pride of Southern cooks," is named for a young lady who sold homemade bread in the streets of England's eighteenth-century spa district. Her type of bread, baked in a tube or fluted tube pan, became very popular in the colonies . . . and it's still popular today!

1 cup warm milk	¼ cup (½ stick) butter,
1 package (0.25 ounce) yeast	melted
¼ cup sugar, divided	3 eggs, beaten
4 cups all-purpose flour	1 teaspoon salt

Place the milk in a small bowl and dissolve the yeast and 1 teaspoon sugar in it; let stand for 5 minutes. In a large bowl, combine the flour, the remaining sugar, the butter, eggs, and salt; mix well. Add the yeast mixture and mix until a dough forms. Place the dough in a 10-inch tube or Bundt pan that has been coated with nonstick baking spray. Cover with plastic wrap and allow the dough to rise in a warm place for 1 hour, or until doubled in size. Remove the plastic wrap and place the bread on the center rack in a cold oven. Bake at 325°F. for 35 to 40 minutes, or until golden. Remove from the oven and allow to cool slightly, then remove to a wire rack to cool completely. Cut and serve.

Note: Although this bread is traditionally baked as a ring in a tube-type pan, it can also be baked in two 9" × 5" loaf pans.

Strawberry Bread

two 9-inch loaves

In a jam for a great-tasting bread? This bread comes to the rescue . . . and with frozen strawberries baked right in, it needs no toppings!

1 package (20 ounces) frozen
   strawberries, thawed and
   mashed
2 cups sugar
1 cup vegetable oil

4 eggs
3 cups self-rising flour,
   divided
1 cup chopped pecans

Preheat the oven to 350°F. In a large bowl, with an electric beater on low speed, beat the strawberries, sugar, oil, and eggs until well mixed. Add 2½ cups flour and continue beating until well combined. In a small bowl, toss the pecans with the remaining ½ cup flour, then stir into the strawberry mixture. Pour into two 9" × 5" loaf pans that have been coated with non-stick baking spray. Bake for 55 to 60 minutes, or until a wooden toothpick inserted into the center comes out clean. Cool slightly, then remove to wire racks to cool completely.

Note: Mixing the flour with the pecans helps to keep the pecans "floating" in the batter so they don't fall to the bottom of the bread when baking.

Plantation Hoecakes

Yup, I'm talking about the garden hoe. You see, years ago, hoes had a use for something other than gardening—they were used to cook these crisp cornmeal cakes over an open fire. Lucky for us, the recipe was developed for indoor ovens!

1½ cups self-rising cornmeal   1½ cups water
¾ cup self-rising flour   About ¾ cup vegetable oil

In a medium-sized bowl, combine all the ingredients except the oil; mix well. Allow the batter to stand for 5 to 10 minutes to thicken slightly. In a large skillet, heat 3 tablespoons oil over medium-high heat. Pour ¼ cup of the batter into the skillet to form each hoecake. Cook for 2 to 3 minutes per side, or until light brown and crisp around the edges. Repeat until all of the batter is used, adding more oil as needed. Serve immediately, or keep warm in a low oven until all the hoecakes are cooked.

Note: These are usually served topped with a little butter. And for a true Southern treat, serve them with molasses.

German Pancakes

Not your traditional pancakes, these are sure to wake everybody up to a sweet aroma that'll bring 'em running!

2 cups all-purpose flour	2 cups milk
2 tablespoons granulated sugar	4 eggs
2 teaspoons baking powder	Vegetable oil for cooking
¼ teaspoon salt	2 tablespoons confectioners' sugar

In a large bowl, combine the flour, granulated sugar, baking powder, and salt; mix well. Whisk the milk and eggs into the flour mixture until smooth. Lightly brush a small skillet with oil, then heat over medium heat until hot but not smoking. Pour ¼ cup of the batter into the skillet, tilting the skillet to coat the bottom evenly with the batter; cook for 2 to 3 minutes, or until firm on top. Turn the pancake, brushing the skillet with additional oil if necessary; cook for about 1 more minute, or until the pancake is light brown on both sides. Fold the pancake in half, then in half again. Remove to a baking sheet and keep warm in a 200°F. oven until ready to serve. Continue with the remaining batter, brushing the skillet with oil as needed. Before serving, sprinkle the pancakes with the confectioners' sugar.

Note: For an even fancier look, top these with fresh, frozen, or canned fruit before sprinkling with the confectioners' sugar.

Cinnamon Bun Pie

8 to 10 servings

Serve this warm for breakfast with coffee, and you're guaranteed to have a great day! Serve it with a scoop of ice cream for your evening dessert, and you're sure to enjoy a load of sweet dreams.

¾ cup plus 2 tablespoons (1¾ sticks) butter, melted, divided
1 cup chopped pecans
½ cup sugar
1 tablespoon ground cinnamon
1 package (17½ ounces) refrigerated flaky biscuits (8 biscuits)

Preheat the oven to 375°F. Coat the bottom of a deep-dish pie plate with 2 tablespoons melted butter; set aside. In a small bowl, combine the pecans, sugar, and cinnamon; mix well. Sprinkle one fourth of the pecan mixture over the bottom of the pie plate. Place the remaining ¾ cup melted butter in a small bowl. Separate each biscuit into 3 layers. Dip the biscuit pieces one at a time in the melted butter, making sure to coat each thoroughly. Layer 8 biscuit pieces in the bottom of the pie plate, completely covering the pecan mixture. Repeat the pecan mixture and biscuit layers 2 more times. Top with the remaining pecan mixture and drizzle with any leftover melted butter. Bake for 20 to 25 minutes, or until the biscuits are golden and cooked through. Allow to cool for 10 minutes, then invert onto a serving platter and slice into wedges. Serve warm.

Note: To enjoy every last bit of pecan flavor, make sure to remove all the pecans from the bottom of the pie plate after inverting and place over the top of the pie before slicing.

The Pickling Jar

Pickles, Relishes, Jams, and Jellies

Half-Sour Dill Pickles

1½ dozen

Good and simple . . . and simply good—just the way we remember them. Every bite is a juicy, crispy, mouthwatering treat!

18 Kirby or other small
   cucumbers (about 2½
   pounds total)
4 cups water

2 cups white vinegar
¼ cup salt
2 tablespoons dried dillweed

Place the cucumbers in a large heat-proof jar; set aside. In a large saucepan, bring the remaining ingredients to a boil over medium-high heat. Pour the vinegar mixture over the cucumbers. Allow to cool completely, then cover and chill overnight before serving.

Note: Remember, don't throw the pickling juices away when the pickles are gone. Just add more cucumbers.

Easy Pickled Beets

about 2 cups

Turn canned beets into homemade pickled beets in no time. And when we team them with fried chicken, we're in for a real treat!

1 can (15 ounces) sliced
   beets, drained
1 small onion, sliced

½ cup white vinegar
3 tablespoons sugar
3 whole cloves

In a medium-sized saucepan, bring all the ingredients to a boil over high heat. Remove from the heat and allow to cool completely. Transfer to an airtight container and chill for at least 4 hours before serving.

Note: If you'd rather, you can finely dice the onions instead of slicing them. Do it whichever way your gang likes best.

Refrigerator Cucumber Pickles

Roll out the barrel . . . and let it keep going, 'cause we use the fridge instead for these crunchy, cool favorites!

3 medium-sized cucumbers,
   thinly sliced
1 medium-sized onion,
   thinly sliced
1 medium-sized green bell
   pepper, coarsely chopped

3 cups sugar
1½ cups white vinegar
3 tablespoons celery seed
1½ teaspoons salt

In a 9" × 13" baking dish, combine the cucumbers, onion, and bell pepper; set aside. In a medium-sized saucepan, bring the remaining ingredients to a boil over medium-high heat, stirring occasionally. Pour the vinegar mixture over the cucumber mixture and allow to cool completely. Cover and chill overnight before serving.

Note: For a little more color, I sometimes use half of a red bell pepper and half of a green one. (It depends what I've got on hand!)

Pickled Jerusalem Artichokes

about 3 cups

In a pickle for what to serve at your next party? Wow 'em with this no-fuss "fancy," and your parties will be the talk of the town!

1 pound Jerusalem
   artichokes, peeled and cut
   into 1-inch chunks (see
   Note)
1 large onion, coarsely
   chopped
2 cups apple cider vinegar
½ cup firmly packed light
   brown sugar
2 teaspoons mustard seed
1 teaspoon turmeric
2 teaspoons salt

In a large saucepan, bring all the ingredients to a boil over high heat. Reduce the heat to medium-low and simmer for 15 minutes. Allow to cool completely, then transfer to an airtight container and chill overnight before serving.

Note: Jerusalem artichokes are different from regular artichokes, but they can also be found in the produce section of your supermarket. They peel with a vegetable peeler as easily as can be.

Pickled Okra

Okra—either you love it or you don't. But before you make up your mind, you've gotta try this pickled version. I bet it'll make fans of you and your family (or at least *some* of you)!

3 cups apple cider vinegar
3 garlic cloves
1 tablespoon chopped fresh
   jalapeño pepper

2 teaspoons dried dillweed
1 teaspoon salt
1 pound fresh okra, trimmed

In a large saucepan, bring all the ingredients except the okra to a boil over high heat. Remove from the heat and add the okra; mix well. Allow to cool completely, then transfer to an airtight container and chill overnight before serving.

Note: I usually like to make this a few days ahead of time so the okra has lots of time to marinate and absorb the flavors of the other ingredients.

Plantation Pickle Chips

about 6 cups

When cucumbers are in abundance, it's time to turn them into the highlight of our relish trays!

4 medium-sized cucumbers, thinly sliced
1 large onion, thinly sliced
1 tablespoon salt
1 cup sugar
1 tablespoon white vinegar

½ teaspoon mustard seed
¼ teaspoon turmeric (optional)
⅛ teaspoon ground cloves
⅛ teaspoon celery seed

In a large bowl, combine the cucumbers, onion, and salt; mix well. Let stand for 1 hour, then drain and place in a large pot. Add the remaining ingredients; mix well. Cover and simmer over low heat for 5 to 6 minutes, or until the cucumbers are slightly tender. Remove from the heat and allow to cool completely. Transfer to an airtight container and chill overnight before serving.

Note: I don't like to peel the cucumbers for these pickles, but you can if you want to.

Carolina Marinated Mushrooms

about 2 cups

The popularity of these tasty goodies is really mushrooming! Why? 'Cause they're so simple to make, they're packed with flavor, *and* they come from the heart of the South!

2 jars (4½ ounces each) whole mushrooms, drained
1 small onion, sliced
⅓ cup red wine vinegar
⅓ cup vegetable oil

1 tablespoon light brown sugar
1 teaspoon prepared yellow mustard

In a medium-sized saucepan, bring all the ingredients to a boil over medium-high heat. Allow to boil for 8 to 10 minutes, or until the onion is tender. Remove from the heat and allow to cool completely. Transfer to an airtight container and chill for at least 4 hours before serving.

Note: Whole mushrooms not available? Use sliced—they work just as well.

Watermelon Rind Pickles

about 2 cups

Yes, watermelon rind! We used to just toss out the rind without giving it a second thought. But now we can make pickles with it that'll have them all saying things like "What *are* these?" and "I can't believe it!"

9 cups water, divided
4 cups 1-inch chunks peeled
   watermelon rind (see Note)
1 cup white vinegar

3½ cups sugar
3 cinnamon sticks
½ teaspoon whole cloves

In a large pot, bring 8 cups water and the watermelon rind to a boil over high heat. Let boil for 15 to 20 minutes, or until the rind is fork-tender. Drain and return the rind to the pot. Add

the remaining 1 cup water, the vinegar, sugar, cinnamon sticks, and cloves and bring to a boil over high heat. Reduce the heat to medium and cook for 35 to 40 minutes, or until the liquid has thickened slightly, stirring frequently. Remove from the heat and allow to cool. Transfer to an airtight container and chill overnight before serving.

Note: To prepare the watermelon rind, cut up a watermelon, separating the sweet pink meat from the white rind. Use a vegetable peeler to peel the green skin off the rind, then cut the rind into 1-inch chunks.

Sweet Pepper Relish

Crunchy and flavorful, this makes a great topper or a simple side dish. Just make sure to set some aside for yourself before you serve it . . . 'cause it goes fast!

4 large bell peppers (2 red and 2 green), finely chopped

2 large onions, finely chopped

1 tablespoon chopped fresh jalapeño pepper

½ cup sugar

½ cup white vinegar

⅓ cup water

In a large saucepan, bring all the ingredients to a boil over medium heat. Cover and allow to boil for 10 minutes, stirring once. Remove from the heat and allow to cool completely. Transfer to an airtight container and chill overnight before serving.

Note: This can be made into a multicolored sweet pepper relish by using 4 colors of bell peppers—one each of red, green, yellow, and orange.

Spiced Grape Relish

about 1½ cups

Deliciously different, this can be served hot or cold as the perfect accent for roast beef or pork!

2 pounds seedless red grapes,
    coarsely chopped
1 cup sugar

¾ cup white vinegar
1 cinnamon stick
1 teaspoon whole cloves

In a large saucepan, bring all the ingredients to a boil over medium-high heat. Allow to boil for 30 to 40 minutes, or until the grapes cook down and the mixture thickens. Remove the cinnamon stick and cloves, and serve the relish warm. Or, if you prefer to serve it cold, allow the relish to cool completely, then transfer to an airtight container and chill for least 4 hours before serving.

Cranberry Surprise Relish

about 5 cups

With the abundance of fruit in the South, it's no wonder that the early settlers made sure to include plenty of tasty combos like this one among their recipes!

2 oranges, cut into large chunks
2 apples, cored and cut into large chunks
1 package (12 ounces) fresh cranberries
1 cup sugar
½ cup pecans

Place all the ingredients in a food processor that has been fitted with its metal cutting blade. Process for 1 to 2 minutes, or until finely chopped and thoroughly mixed, scraping down the sides of the container as needed. Serve immediately, or transfer to an airtight container and chill until ready to serve.

Note: There's no need to peel the oranges, 'cause we actually want bits of peel in this relish. If you want to use frozen cranberries, make sure to thaw them before processing.

Tomato Relish

What a super way to use up our harvest of tomatoes. And with the addition of a few off-the-shelf ingredients, this relish is ready in no time!

4 large tomatoes, chopped
1 large onion, chopped
2 tablespoons chopped fresh
   jalapeño peppers

½ cup sugar
½ cup white vinegar
2 teaspoons salt

In a large pot, combine all the ingredients over medium heat; mix well. Cook for 30 to 35 minutes, or until thickened, stirring occasionally. Remove from the heat and allow to cool completely. Transfer to an airtight container and chill overnight before serving.

Note: I like to add a little more jalapeño pepper for a really zippy relish.

Spiced Peaches

about 4 cups

With peaches grown in such abundance in the South, it's no wonder this refreshing side dish is the perfect go-along for chicken or pork.

1 can (29 ounces) peach halves, drained, syrup reserved
1 cup water
½ cup white vinegar

1 cup sugar
½ cup red-hot cinnamon candies
6 whole cloves

In a large saucepan, bring the reserved peach syrup, the water, vinegar, sugar, cinnamon candies, and cloves to a boil over medium-high heat. Allow to boil until the cinnamon candies melt. Add the peaches and return to a boil. Reduce the heat to low and simmer for 4 to 5 minutes, or until the edges of the peaches turn red. Remove from the heat and allow to cool completely. Transfer to an airtight container and chill for at least 4 hours before serving.

Note: This one's perfect as a side dish at practically any meal, or as part of a sweet relish tray.

Spiced Pineapple

about 1 cup

The secret here is the red-hot candies. Yup, that's what gives this condiment its special flavor!

1 can (20 ounces) pineapple
   chunks in heavy syrup,
   drained, syrup reserved
1 cup water

¾ cup white vinegar
¼ cup red-hot cinnamon
   candies
6 whole cloves

In a large saucepan, bring the reserved pineapple syrup, the water, vinegar, cinnamon candies, and cloves to a boil over high heat. Allow to boil until the cinnamon candies melt, stirring constantly. Add the pineapple and return to a boil. Allow to boil for 25 to 30 minutes, or until the pineapple is slightly translucent and most of the liquid has evaporated, stirring occasionally. Remove from the heat and allow to cool completely. Transfer to an airtight container and chill for at least 4 hours before serving.

Note: You know this is done when the pineapple is glazed and looks candied.

Blue Ribbon Strawberry Preserves

about 3 cups

When it comes to jams, jellies, and preserves, the folks in the South really know how to win blue ribbons!

1 quart fresh strawberries, washed, hulled, and quartered

3 cups sugar
1 tablespoon lemon juice

In a large saucepan, bring all the ingredients to a boil over medium heat, stirring constantly. Reduce the heat to low and simmer for 10 to 12 minutes, or until the strawberries have cooked down and the mixture has thickened, stirring frequently. Remove from the heat and allow to cool completely. Transfer to an airtight container and chill for at least 4 hours before serving.

Note: If you start with really sweet strawberries you can decrease the amount of sugar to between 2 and 2½ cups, if you want.

Peach Marmalade

about 4 cups

You'll get a real kick out of the taste of this fruity spread. Oh, don't worry about the alcohol in the bourbon—it cooks off, leaving a rich, smooth accent in the marmalade.

2 packages (20 ounces each)   2 cups sugar
   frozen peaches, thawed   1 cup bourbon (see Note)

In a large saucepan, bring all the ingredients to a boil over medium-high heat, stirring constantly. Reduce the heat to medium-low and simmer for 30 to 40 minutes, or until the peaches have broken down and the syrup has thickened, stirring occasionally. Remove from the heat and allow to cool completely. Transfer to an airtight container and chill for at least 4 hours before serving.

Note: Even though the alcohol in the bourbon cooks off, if you'd prefer, you can substitute water for the bourbon.

Pepper Jelly

about 6 cups

Perfectly spicy *and* sweet—just the way I like it.

2 medium-sized green bell peppers, chopped

14 fresh jalapeño peppers (about ½ pound total), stems and seeds removed, chopped

7 cups sugar

1¼ cups apple cider vinegar

⅓ cup apple juice

1 package (6 ounces) liquid pectin (see Note)

¼ teaspoon green food color (optional)

In a large pot, combine all the ingredients except the pectin and food color. Bring to a boil over medium heat and allow to boil for 2 to 3 minutes. Add the pectin, then return the mixture to a boil and boil for 2 to 3 minutes, stirring constantly. Remove from the heat and strain, discarding the pepper pieces. Place in a large bowl and add the food color, if desired; mix until well blended. Pour into airtight containers, cover, and allow to jell at room temperature. Store in the refrigerator until ready to use.

Note: Liquid pectin can be found in the supermarket produce or baking section, or near the jellies and jams. This can be stored in the refrigerator for several months.

The Soup Pot

Soups, Chowders, Gumbos, and Stews

Irish Potato Soup

6 to 8 servings

Many years ago, when you said "potatoes" to Southerners, they'd automatically think of sweet potatoes 'cause they were a traditional Southern favorite, but white or "Irish" potato dishes like this one have also been Southern specialties.

2 tablespoons butter
1 small onion, chopped
1 celery stalk, chopped
6 medium-sized potatoes, peeled and diced
2 cans (10½ ounces each) condensed chicken broth
2 cups plus 3 tablespoons water, divided
1 teaspoon Worcestershire sauce
¼ teaspoon dried thyme
¼ teaspoon black pepper
2 tablespoons cornstarch

In a soup pot, melt the butter over medium heat and sauté the onion and celery for 3 to 4 minutes, or until tender. Add the potatoes, broth, 2 cups water, the Worcestershire sauce, thyme, and pepper; mix well. Bring to a boil over medium-high heat, then reduce the heat to low and simmer for 35 minutes. In a small bowl, combine the remaining 3 tablespoons water and the cornstarch; stir into the soup and cook until thickened.

Note: Top with thin slices of hard-boiled eggs and sprinkle with chopped fresh parsley just before serving.

Butter Bean and Ham Soup

8 to 10 servings

Wanna get everyone's attention? Top each bowlful of this with crispy homemade croutons. And to be really Southern, make croutons with cubes of leftover corn bread that you toss with butter and toast in the oven. Oh, what a classic!

2 cans (14½ ounces each) ready-to-use chicken broth
1 package (16 ounces) frozen butter beans, thawed (see Note)
1 can (28 ounces) diced tomatoes, undrained
1 can (15 ounces) sliced potatoes, drained
1 can (8¼ ounces) sliced carrots, drained
½ pound cooked ham, diced (see Note)
1 small onion, chopped
¼ teaspoon black pepper

In a soup pot, combine all the ingredients and bring to a boil over medium-high heat. Reduce the heat to low and simmer for 30 minutes to allow the flavors to marry and the soup to thicken.

Note: Sure, you can use two drained 16-ounce cans of butter beans in place of the frozen ones. And, for the ham, use leftovers or get ½ pound thick-cut ham from the deli and dice that up. Go with whatever you've got on hand.

Tomato-Vegetable Soup

8 to 10 servings

Originally this soup was made with fresh-from-the-farm veggies—and let me tell you, that's the best. But with today's busy lifestyles, we can enjoy it year-round by using a few conveniences. As for the taste, well, let's just say that all the bowls on the table are always emptied!

2 cans (15 ounces each) whole or sliced potatoes, drained and coarsely chopped

2 cans (14½ ounces each) ready-to-use beef broth

1 can (28 ounces) tomato purée

1 can (14½ ounces) green beans, drained

1 package (16 ounces) frozen gumbo vegetable mix, thawed (see Note)

2 large tomatoes, quartered

1 small onion, chopped

2 tablespoons Worcestershire sauce

2 tablespoons butter

1 teaspoon salt

1 teaspoon black pepper

In a soup pot, combine all the ingredients and bring to a boil over medium-high heat. Reduce the heat to medium-low and cook for 40 to 45 minutes, or until the vegetables are tender and the soup has thickened, stirring occasionally.

Note: Frozen gumbo vegetable mix will include vegetables like corn, squash, and okra, and can be found in the frozen vegetable section of the supermarket. If unavailable, substitute one 10-ounce package of frozen corn and one 10-ounce package of frozen okra.

Potato-Cheese Soup

4 to 6 servings

Nothing beats this popular restaurant favorite for the comforting tastes we all crave. And now we can have it at home anytime we want!

2 tablespoons butter
4 cups frozen cubed hash brown potatoes (half of a 2-pound package), thawed
1 medium-sized onion, finely chopped
1 tablespoon all-purpose flour

4 cups (1 quart) milk
1 container (3 ounces) real bacon bits
½ teaspoon salt
¼ teaspoon black pepper
2 cups (8 ounces) shredded sharp Cheddar cheese

In a soup pot, melt the butter over medium heat. Add the potatoes and onions and sauté for 5 to 7 minutes, or until tender. Add the flour, stirring until the vegetables are well coated. Add the milk, bacon bits, salt, and pepper; mix well. Cook for 20 minutes, stirring occasionally. Stir in the cheese and cook for 5 to 7 minutes, or until the cheese has melted. Serve immediately.

Note: Serve this with Cheese Biscuits (page 6) for an extra-cheesy appetizer or light lunch.

Oyster-Brie Soup

Oysters are a lively staple of the South. Why, just look on any restaurant menu from Charleston, South Carolina, to Norfolk, Virginia, and you'll probably find some version of oyster soup or bisque.

1 large onion, chopped
1 celery stalk, chopped
2 tablespoons all-purpose flour
¼ teaspoon cayenne pepper
2 tablespoons butter
2 cups hot water
½ cup dry white wine

1 container (16 ounces) sour cream
1 pound Brie, cut into 1-inch chunks
3 containers (8 ounces each) shucked fresh oysters, rinsed and drained (see Note)

In a medium-sized bowl, combine the onion, celery, flour, and cayenne pepper. In a soup pot, melt the butter over medium heat and add the onion mixture; sauté for 5 to 7 minutes, or until the vegetables are tender. Add the remaining ingredients and cook for 12 to 15 minutes, or until the Brie has melted and the oysters are firm and cooked through, stirring frequently.

Note: Remember to rinse the oysters well to remove any sand particles. And if the oysters happen to be large, cut them in half before adding them to the soup.

Salmon-Dill Chowder

Everybody says that location is everything—and the South boasts a super coastline that's brimming with fish! My fresh catch of today is this salmon-based chowder that's "reely" good!

6 cups milk
2 cans (14¾ ounces each) red
  salmon, drained and flaked
  (skin and bones discarded)
2 medium-sized potatoes,
  peeled and diced

1 small onion, chopped
2 tablespoons butter
1 teaspoon dried dillweed
1 teaspoon salt
¼ teaspoon black pepper

In a soup pot, combine all the ingredients and bring to a boil over medium heat, stirring occasionally. Reduce the heat to low and simmer for 20 to 25 minutes, or until the potatoes are tender, stirring occasionally.

Note: If fresh dill is available, use 1 tablespoon chopped dill instead of the dried, and don't forget to garnish the finished soup with a bit more.

Fill-'Em-Up Fish Chowder

No way—this isn't simply a bowl of soup you have *before* dinner. . . . It's a whole meal in a bowl!

¼ cup (½ stick) butter
¼ pound sliced deli ham, finely chopped
2 celery stalks, chopped
1 large onion, chopped
2 cans (14½ ounces each) ready-to-use chicken broth
4 large potatoes, peeled and diced
½ teaspoon paprika

½ teaspoon dried thyme
¼ teaspoon cayenne pepper
¼ teaspoon salt
4 cups (1 quart) milk, divided
2 pounds fresh or frozen white-fleshed fish fillets, such as cod, haddock, or whiting, thawed if frozen, cut into large chunks
3 tablespoons cornstarch

In a soup pot, melt the butter over medium-high heat. Add the ham, celery, and onion and sauté for 8 to 10 minutes, or until the onion is tender. Add the broth, potatoes, paprika, thyme, cayenne pepper, and salt and bring to a boil. Allow to boil for 10 to 12 minutes, or until the potatoes are tender, stirring occasionally. Add 3½ cups milk and the fish and return to a low boil. Allow to boil for 5 to 7 minutes, or until the fish is cooked through. In a small bowl, whisk together the cornstarch and the remaining ½ cup milk until well blended. Stir into the chowder and simmer until thickened.

Note: This is usually served topped with ketchup and with oyster crackers on the side.

Tomato-Crab Bisque

8 to 10 servings

It's fun to impress company at the dinner table, but who needs to do a lot of work? This one's from my "tried and true" file, 'cause it's as easy as it is elegant!

2 tablespoons butter
2 large onions, finely
   chopped
2 celery stalks, finely
   chopped
1 can (28 ounces) crushed
   tomatoes

4 cups (1 quart) half-and-half
2 chicken bouillon cubes
1 teaspoon salt
1 teaspoon black pepper
3 cans (6½ ounces each)
   crabmeat, drained

In a soup pot, melt the butter over medium heat. Add the onions and celery and sauté for 4 to 5 minutes, or until tender. Add the crushed tomatoes, half-and-half, bouillon cubes, salt, and pepper. Cook for 5 to 7 minutes, or until hot but not boiling, stirring occasionally. Stir in the crabmeat and cook for 2 to 3 minutes, or until heated through.

Hearty Chicken Gumbo

6 to 8 servings

A gumbo is really just a hearty Cajun stew. So when we need to serve something to chase away the cold-weather blues, this one's sure to stick to our ribs!

1 pound bacon, chopped
1½ pounds boneless, skinless chicken breasts, cut into 1-inch chunks
1½ pounds boneless, skinless chicken thighs, cut into 1-inch chunks
1 can (28 ounces) diced tomatoes, undrained
1 can (15¼ ounces) whole kernel corn, drained
1 package (16 ounces) frozen cut okra, thawed
2 cans (14½ ounces each) ready-to-use chicken broth
1 teaspoon salt
1 teaspoon black pepper

In a soup pot, cook the bacon over medium heat for 10 to 12 minutes, or until golden, stirring occasionally; drain off the fat. Add the remaining ingredients and bring to a boil. Allow to boil for 35 to 40 minutes, or until the chicken is no longer pink and the gumbo has thickened, stirring occasionally.

Note: To add a Louisiana flavor to the gumbo, add some hot pepper sauce just before serving.

Fourth of July Hash

8 to 10 servings

Firehouse fund-raisers are a Southern tradition on the Fourth of July and you can always count on chicken simmering over a glowing fire in a screened-in room off the back of the firehouse!

2 cups water
1½ pounds boneless, skinless
  chicken breasts
1½ pounds boneless, skinless
  chicken thighs
1 pound pork stew meat,
  trimmed
1 pound beef stew meat,
  trimmed
6 medium-sized potatoes,
  peeled and quartered

3 medium-sized onions,
  quartered
½ cup (1 stick) butter
1½ teaspoons salt
1½ teaspoons black pepper
1 cup ketchup
1 can (12 ounces) evaporated
  milk

In a soup pot, bring all the ingredients except the ketchup and evaporated milk to a boil over high heat. Reduce the heat to medium, cover, and allow to boil for 40 to 45 minutes, or until the chicken and meats are tender, stirring occasionally. In a food processor that has been fitted with its metal cutting blade, process the mixture from the pot in batches until finely chopped. Return the hash to the pot. Add the ketchup and evaporated milk; mix well. Cover loosely and cook for 15 to 20 minutes, or until heated through, stirring occasionally.

Note: For an authentic Southern hash dinner, serve with rice, white bread, and plenty of pickles.

Brunswick Stew

There are lots of stories about where Brunswick stew originated. Many folks say its roots are Virginian, while others swear it's from Georgia. I'll tell ya, what I care about most is that it comes bubbling out of the pot, tasty as can be!

5 cups water
2 cans (10½ ounces each) condensed chicken broth
2 pounds pork stew meat, trimmed
1 pound beef stew meat, trimmed
1 can (15 ounces) cream-style corn
1 can (14½ ounces) whole tomatoes, undrained

2 medium-sized baking potatoes, quartered
1 large onion, coarsely chopped
¼ teaspoon cayenne pepper
2 cups ketchup
¼ cup white vinegar
2 tablespoons Worcestershire sauce

In a soup pot, combine the water, broth, pork, beef, corn, tomatoes, potatoes, onion, and cayenne pepper; bring to a boil over high heat. Reduce the heat to medium-low and simmer for 60 to 70 minutes, or until the meat and potatoes are tender, stirring occasionally. In a food processor that has been fitted with its metal cutting blade, process the stew in batches until finely chopped. Return the stew to the pot and add the remaining ingredients. Cook over medium heat for 5 to 6 minutes, or until well combined and heated through.

Creamy Oven-Baked Beef Stew

6 to 8 servings

Since the proof of the pudding is in the eating, everybody loves this creamy stew made with a secret ingredient—tapioca!

2 pounds beef stew meat, trimmed
4 medium-sized potatoes, cut into 1-inch chunks
6 medium-sized carrots, cut into ½-inch chunks
1 medium-sized onion, chopped
2 cups tomato juice
1 cup water
3 tablespoons quick-cooking tapioca
1 teaspoon sugar
2 teaspoons salt
½ teaspoon black pepper

Preheat the oven to 350°F. In a 9" × 13" baking dish that has been coated with nonstick cooking spray, combine the beef, potatoes, carrots, and onion; mix well. In a large bowl, combine the remaining ingredients; mix well. Pour the tomato juice mixture over the beef and vegetables. Cover tightly with aluminum foil and bake for 2 to 2¼ hours, or until the beef and vegetables are tender.

Note: This is the perfect dish for when you want to prepare dinner ahead of time. Just put it together, cover, and chill. Begin to bake it 2½ to 3 hours before serving.

Wintry Chicken Stew

6 to 8 servings

When the cold winds are howling and we need to warm up, what could be better than a hot 'n' hearty bowl of stew chock-full of everybody's favorite—chicken!

One 3- to 3½-pound chicken, cut into 8 pieces (see Note)
4 medium-sized baking potatoes, peeled and quartered
1 large onion, chopped
3 cups water
1 can (28 ounces) whole tomatoes, drained and quartered, juice reserved

1 can (15 ounces) cream-style corn
½ cup long- or whole-grain rice
2 tablespoons butter
1½ teaspoons salt
1 teaspoon black pepper
1 cup (½ pint) heavy cream

In a soup pot, combine all the ingredients except the heavy cream and bring to a boil over high heat, stirring occasionally. Reduce the heat to medium-low and simmer for 45 to 50 minutes, or until the chicken is fork-tender, stirring occasionally. Stir in the cream and cook for 2 to 3 minutes, or until heated through.

Note: If you prefer, remove the chicken meat from the bones before serving. It's easier to eat that way.

Frogmore Stew

4 to 6 servings

Frogmore stew is the clambake of the South. Cover the table with newspaper, then boil this up and dump it out. But make sure you save the broth for dunking!

8 cups water
2 tablespoons seafood
  seasoning
¼ teaspoon cayenne pepper
½ teaspoon salt
1 pound kielbasa sausage,
  cut into 2-inch pieces
6 medium-sized potatoes,
  cut in half

6 medium-sized onions,
  cut in half
3 ears corn, husked and cut
  into 3-inch pieces
1 pound large shrimp,
  unpeeled

In a soup pot, combine the water, seafood seasoning, cayenne pepper, and salt. Bring to a boil over high heat and add the sausage, potatoes, onions, and corn. Cook for 15 to 20 minutes, or until the potatoes are fork-tender. Add the shrimp and cook for 2 to 3 minutes, or until the shrimp are pink and cooked through. Strain the stew and serve immediately, along with bowls of the broth for dunking.

Southern Beef Stew

5 to 6 servings

One-pot meals are great for chilly weather, so what could be better than the comforting taste of an old favorite made Southern-style with a surprise ingredient—coffee?!

3 tablespoons all-purpose flour	2 teaspoons salt
2 pounds beef stew meat, trimmed	1 teaspoon black pepper
¼ cup (½ stick) butter	6 medium-sized potatoes, peeled and quartered
2 cups water	6 carrots, cut into large chunks
1 cup black coffee	3 medium-sized onions, quartered
1 teaspoon dried thyme	

Place the flour in a shallow dish; add the beef chunks and coat completely with the flour. In a soup pot, melt the butter over medium-high heat and cook the beef for 8 to 10 minutes, turning to brown all sides. Add the water, coffee, thyme, salt, and pepper; mix well and bring to a boil. Reduce the heat to low, cover, and simmer for 1 hour. Add the remaining ingredients and simmer for 50 to 60 minutes, or until the beef and vegetables are tender, stirring occasionally.

Country Seafood Stew

In the South, the garnish is just as important as the soup, so make sure you top each bowl with very thin slices of lemon. Not only will you see the difference, you'll taste it!

One (4-ounce) piece salt pork, skin removed and cut into ½-inch chunks

2 medium-sized onions, coarsely chopped

1 can (28 ounces) whole tomatoes, drained and quartered, juice reserved

1 can (15 ounces) tomato sauce

1 can (6 ounces) tomato paste

2 tablespoons Worcestershire sauce

½ teaspoon black pepper

1 pound fresh or frozen white-fleshed fish fillets, such as cod, haddock, or whiting, thawed if frozen, cut into large chunks

1 pound large shrimp, peeled and deveined

In a soup pot, cook the salt pork over medium heat for 5 to 6 minutes, or until golden brown. Add the onions and sauté for 3 to 4 minutes, or until tender. Add the tomatoes with their juice, the tomato sauce, tomato paste, Worcestershire sauce, and pepper; bring to a boil. Add the fish; mix well. Reduce the heat to medium-low, cover, and simmer for 20 minutes; add the shrimp and cook for 10 minutes, or until the shrimp is cooked.

Note: Serve with lots of rice so you can enjoy every last spoonful of stew. It's a heartier meal that way, too.

Oyster Supreme Stew

If you've never tried this, now's the perfect time. Rich and creamy, this seafood stew is truly supreme!

8 cups (½ gallon) milk
½ cup (1 stick) butter
2 containers (8 ounces each)
   shucked fresh oysters,
   rinsed and drained
   (see Note, page 45)

2 teaspoons salt
1 teaspoon black pepper

In a soup pot, combine the milk and butter and heat over medium heat for 3 to 4 minutes, or until the butter is melted. Add the remaining ingredients and cook for 4 to 6 minutes, or until the oysters are firm and cooked through and the stew is hot.

Note: I think that oyster crackers must have been invented to go along with this stew! Even if they weren't, I still like to serve plenty of them with it.

Satisfying Salmon Stew

6 to 8 servings

No need to go fishing—canned salmon goes swimmingly with this recipe. Serve it piping hot with crusty bread and a fresh garden salad for a satisfying meal anytime!

6 cups milk
2 cans (14¾ ounces each) red salmon, drained and flaked (skin and bones discarded)
2 large baking potatoes, peeled and finely chopped

1 medium-sized onion, finely chopped
¼ cup (½ stick) butter
½ teaspoon salt
¼ teaspoon black pepper
½ cup instant potato flakes

In a soup pot, combine all the ingredients except the potato flakes over medium-low heat. Simmer for 20 to 25 minutes, or until the vegetables are tender. Stir the potato flakes into the stew and cook until thickened.

Note: For a flavorful finishing touch, top each bowl of stew with very thin slices of lemon.

Shortcut Seafood Stew

4 to 6 servings

All right, I'll admit it—I cheated. I used a few shortcuts here that cut the cooking time of the original recipe by one third. But one thing I didn't cheat on is the flavor.

¼ cup (½ stick) butter
½ of a small green bell
   pepper, chopped
2 garlic cloves, minced
1 pound smoked sausage
   such as kielbasa, coarsely
   chopped
1 pound large shrimp, peeled
   and deveined
1 container (12 ounces)
   brown gravy

2 cups water, divided
¼ teaspoon dried basil
¼ teaspoon dried thyme
½ teaspoon black pepper
1 container (8 ounces)
   shucked fresh oysters,
   rinsed and drained
   (see Notes on this page
   and page 45)
2 tablespoons cornstarch

In a soup pot, melt the butter over medium-high heat and sauté the green pepper and garlic for 3 to 4 minutes, or until the bell pepper is tender. Add the sausage and shrimp; sauté for 5 to 6 minutes, or until the shrimp turn pink. Add the gravy, 1½ cups water, the basil, thyme, and black pepper; mix well and bring to a boil. Reduce the heat to low, add the oysters, and simmer for 15 minutes. In a small bowl, combine the remaining ½ cup water and the cornstarch. Stir in and cook until thickened.

Note: If you prefer, you can use 2 drained 10-ounce cans of baby clams instead of the oysters.

The Salad Bar

Chilled Salads and Gelatin Molds

Make-Ahead Refrigerator Salad

A lettuce salad that we can make ahead of time? Sure! Wanna know how we do that without it wilting? The trick is in the layers—the ingredients don't really get mixed together till we toss the salad just before serving!

2 cups mayonnaise
½ cup sour cream
½ teaspoon garlic powder
1 medium-sized head iceberg lettuce, chopped
2 large red bell peppers, finely chopped
1 medium-sized onion, finely chopped

1 package (9 ounces) frozen green peas, thawed
3 celery stalks, finely chopped
2 cups (8 ounces) shredded sharp Cheddar cheese
1 container (3 ounces) real bacon bits

In a medium-sized bowl, combine the mayonnaise, sour cream, and garlic powder; mix well. In a large glass bowl, layer half of the lettuce, then half of the red peppers, onion, green peas, celery, mayonnaise mixture, and cheese. Repeat the layers once more, then top with the bacon bits. Cover and chill for at least 2 hours before serving. Toss just before serving.

Note: Using a trifle dish or large glass bowl with straight sides allows us to see all the colorful layers of the salad.

Vinegar Slaw

I was lucky enough to get this recipe from an aunt of one of my Southern friends. And am I glad, 'cause this version of coleslaw is a nice change from the old standby mayo kind.

1 cup sugar
¾ cup white vinegar
¾ cup vegetable oil
½ teaspoon salt

¼ teaspoon black pepper
2 packages (16 ounces each)
    shredded green cabbage

In a medium-sized saucepan, combine the sugar, vinegar, oil, salt, and pepper over medium-high heat. Bring to a boil, stirring until the sugar has dissolved. Remove from the heat and allow to cool. Place the cabbage in a large bowl and add the vinegar mixture, tossing until well coated. Cover and chill for at least 2 hours before serving.

Sweet Relish-Potato Salad

6 to 8 servings

When I was a kid, my mom used to make potato salad and store it in mayonnaise jars in the fridge. That way, when it was time for our Sunday afternoon picnic in the country, the salad was ready to travel . . . along with me and my sister. I bet Dad would have liked it if this Southern-style salad had been packed in those jars!

6 medium-sized baking potatoes
1 cup mayonnaise
4 hard-boiled eggs, sliced
1 small onion, chopped
2 celery stalks, diced

½ cup sweet pickle relish, drained
1 jar (2 ounces) chopped pimientos, drained
½ teaspoon salt
½ teaspoon black pepper

Place the potatoes in a large pot and add enough water to cover them. Bring to a boil over high heat and cook for 20 to 25 minutes, or until fork-tender. Drain and allow to cool. Cut into chunks and place in a large bowl. Add the remaining ingredients and combine until well mixed. Cover and chill for at least 2 hours before serving.

Picnic Egg Salad

4 to 6 servings

All egg salads aren't created equal! With the zest of lemon and the zing of cayenne pepper, this one is so refreshingly different that it's easy to see why it wins over the hearts of Southerners again and again.

12 eggs	¼ teaspoon cayenne pepper
½ cup mayonnaise	¾ teaspoon salt
1 teaspoon grated lemon peel	¼ teaspoon white pepper

Place the eggs in a large saucepan and add enough water to cover them; bring to a boil over high heat. When the water begins to boil, remove the saucepan from the heat, cover, and let sit for 20 minutes. Drain off the hot water and run cold water over the eggs. Add some ice cubes to the water and let the eggs cool for 5 to 10 minutes. Peel the eggs, then finely chop in a large bowl. Add the remaining ingredients and mix until well blended. Cover and chill for at least 1 hour before serving.

Curried Chicken Salad

6 to 8 servings

I'm a true chicken salad lover, and when it's made with a bit of curry and lemon juice, we're in for a really special meal!

¾ cup mayonnaise
¼ cup sour cream
1 teaspoon lemon juice
1 teaspoon curry powder
1 teaspoon salt

6 cups chunked cooked
  chicken
½ cup pecans, coarsely
  chopped

In a large bowl, combine the mayonnaise, sour cream, lemon juice, curry powder, and salt; mix well. Add the chicken and pecans and mix until thoroughly coated. Cover and chill for at least 2 hours before serving.

Note: When I'm grilling chicken, I like to grill some extra boneless, skinless chicken breasts so I have them for this salad. I love the grilled flavor, but you can cook the chicken any way you like.

Cucumber Salad

4 to 6 servings

Try a spoon or two of this on a tossed green salad, or as a chilled side salad to showcase those abundant summer cukes!

2 medium-sized cucumbers,
   peeled and thinly sliced
1 tablespoon salt
3 cups ice water
4 scallions, thinly sliced
½ of a small green bell
   pepper, chopped

¼ cup sour cream
2 tablespoons white vinegar
2 tablespoons sugar
⅛ teaspoon black pepper

In a large bowl, combine the cucumbers, salt, and ice water. Cover and chill for 1 hour, then drain and return the cucumbers to the bowl. Add the remaining ingredients and mix until well combined. Cover and chill for at least 2 hours before serving.

Note: The ice-cold salted water helps make the cukes extra crispy!

Summer's Best Broccoli Salad

6 to 8 servings

This summery salad is the cream of the crop! It's the perfect way to add veggies to our lunch or dinner.

1½ cups mayonnaise
½ cup sour cream
¼ cup sugar
1 bunch broccoli, cut into small florets (see Note)
½ head cauliflower, cut into small florets (see Note)

1 small red onion, chopped
1 cup (4 ounces) shredded sharp Cheddar cheese
1 container (3 ounces) real bacon bits

In a large bowl, combine the mayonnaise, sour cream, and sugar; mix well. Add the remaining ingredients, mixing until well combined. Cover and chill for at least 4 hours before serving.

Note: Make sure to cut the broccoli and cauliflower into very small florets. This is even better if it's made a few days ahead of time and allowed to marinate in the fridge.

Zippy Sauerkraut Salad

Super for summer picnics and barbecues, this zippy salad gives new life to plain old sauerkraut!

1 can (27 ounces) sauerkraut, drained
1 jar (2 ounces) chopped pimientos, drained
1 medium-sized green bell pepper, chopped

1 small onion, finely chopped
4 celery stalks, chopped
1 cup sugar

In a large bowl, combine all the ingredients; mix well. Cover and chill for at least 2 hours before serving.

Three-Bean Salad

10 to 12 servings

If you're saying, "So, what's the big deal about making three-bean salad?" you're right—making it is no big deal . . . but the taste of this one is *very* big!

1 can (14 ounces) sweetened condensed milk
1 cup sour cream
¼ cup prepared yellow mustard
3 tablespoons lemon juice
1 teaspoon garlic powder
½ teaspoon salt

2 cans (19 ounces each) red kidney beans, drained
2 cans (16 ounces each) yellow wax beans, drained
2 cans (16 ounces each) cut green beans, drained
4 celery stalks, chopped
1 small onion, chopped

In a large bowl, combine the sweetened condensed milk, sour cream, mustard, lemon juice, garlic powder, and salt; mix well. Add the remaining ingredients and toss until well combined. Cover and chill for at least 2 hours before serving.

Note: If you make this the night before serving, make sure to drain some of the liquid from the salad just before serving, 'cause the beans will release water as they sit.

Perfect Pea Salad

3 to 4 servings

So thick and creamy delicious that it can be a salad, a spread, a sandwich filling. You name it—it's "eggs-actly" perfect!

1 tablespoon butter
½ cup mayonnaise
1 can (15 ounces) peas,
   drained

3 hard-boiled eggs, finely
   chopped
¼ teaspoon salt
⅛ teaspoon black pepper

In a small saucepan, melt the butter over medium-low heat. Add the mayonnaise and peas and toss quickly to coat; remove from the heat. Transfer to a medium-sized bowl and add the remaining ingredients; mix until well combined. Cover and chill for at least 2 hours before serving.

Waldorf Salad

6 to 8 servings

Even a classic Waldorf salad can take on a Southern accent with the addition of a few green grapes and the crunch of pecans.

4 large apples, cored and cut into 1-inch chunks
3 celery stalks, chopped
1 cup seedless green grapes

½ cup coarsely chopped pecans
¾ cup mayonnaise
2 teaspoons lemon juice

In a large bowl, combine all the ingredients and toss until mixed and the fruit and nuts are well coated. Serve, or cover and chill until ready to serve.

Plantation Fruit Salad

10 to 12 servings

It's no wonder this was a popular snack on the plantations of the Deep South. Even before we had refrigeration, everyone enjoyed the cool, refreshing taste of fresh fruit! And today, we still love these same flavors . . . with a few little extras thrown in!

4 large Red Delicious apples, cored and cut into bite-sized pieces
4 oranges, peeled and sectioned
4 bananas, cut into bite-sized pieces

2 pears, cored and cut into bite-sized pieces
½ cup coarsely chopped pecans
½ cup maraschino cherries, quartered
1 cup mayonnaise

In a large bowl, combine all the ingredients except the mayonnaise. Add the mayonnaise and gently mix to coat the fruit pieces. Cover and chill for at least 2 hours before serving.

Chilled Creamy Pears

I've always loved the team of fruit and cheese. How 'bout you? Now, this combination may be a bit untraditional, but, boy, it's good and refreshing!

⅓ cup mayonnaise
1 package (3 ounces) cream
  cheese, softened
6 romaine lettuce leaves
1 can (29 ounces) pear
  halves, well drained

¼ cup (1 ounce) finely
  shredded sharp Cheddar
  cheese

In a small bowl, combine the mayonnaise and cream cheese; mix well. Line a serving plate with the lettuce leaves, then place the pear halves over the lettuce. Spoon the cream cheese mixture equally into the pears. Sprinkle with the Cheddar cheese and serve, or cover loosely and chill until ready to serve.

Nutty Pineapple-Lime Mold

12 to 16 servings

Here in the South, gelatin salads have always been popular. They're portable enough to take to a potluck supper, and they keep well in our warm weather!

2 packages (4 servings each)
  lime-flavored gelatin
1 cup hot water
1 package (8 ounces) cream
  cheese, softened
1 can (12 ounces) evaporated
  milk

1 can (20 ounces) crushed
  pineapple, drained
1 cup chopped pecans
1 cup miniature
  marshmallows

In a large bowl, dissolve the gelatin in the hot water. Add the cream cheese and, with an electric beater on low speed, beat for 4 to 5 minutes, or until well mixed. Add the remaining ingredients and stir until combined. Spoon into a 1½-quart mold or bowl, cover, and chill for at least 4 hours, or until set. When ready to serve, if using a mold, dip the bottom of the mold in warm water for a few seconds, then invert quickly onto a serving plate larger than the mold. Shake gently to loosen from the mold.

Strawberry Patch Salad

6 to 9 servings

Cool, creamy, light, and full of fruit, this is one of those recipes that you find yourself eating morning, noon, and night.

1 package (4-serving size) strawberry-flavored gelatin
1 cup boiling water
1 package (10 ounces) frozen sweetened strawberries in syrup, thawed, undrained
1 can (8 ounces) crushed pineapple, drained
1 ripe banana, mashed
½ cup chopped pecans
1 cup reduced-fat sour cream

In a large bowl, dissolve the gelatin in the boiling water. Stir in the strawberries and their syrup, the pineapple, banana, and pecans until well mixed. Spoon half of the mixture into an 8-inch square baking dish and chill for about 1 hour, or until set; reserve the remaining gelatin mixture at room temperature. When the chilled gelatin is set, spread the top with the sour cream, then top with the reserved gelatin mixture. Cover and chill for at least 3 hours before serving.

Pineapple-Carrot Salad

6 to 8 servings

For that afternoon luncheon on the porch, don't forget this colorful salad that has "grate" taste appeal!

1 package (4-serving size) lemon-flavored gelatin
1 cup boiling water
1 can (20 ounces) crushed pineapple, drained, 1 cup juice reserved (see Note)

1 teaspoon grated orange peel
1 cup grated carrots

In a large bowl, dissolve the gelatin in the boiling water. Add the reserved pineapple juice and the orange peel; mix well. Chill for 8 to 10 minutes, or until slightly thickened. Stir in the pineapple and carrots. Cover and chill in the bowl, or pour into a gelatin mold, cover, and chill for at least 4 hours, or until set. If using a mold, when ready to serve, dip the bottom of the mold in warm water for a few seconds, then invert quickly onto a serving plate larger than the mold. Shake gently to loosen from the mold.

Note: Depending on the brand of crushed pineapple you use, the amount of juice may vary. If you have less than 1 cup, just add enough cold water to it to yield 1 cup.

Cherry-Cola Salad

12 to 16 servings

Put this on your list to take to your next family reunion—and you're sure to get all the raves! The gang will want reunions more often!

1 can (20 ounces) crushed pineapple in heavy syrup, drained, syrup reserved
1 can (16½ ounces) Bing cherries in heavy syrup, drained and chopped, syrup reserved

2 packages (4 servings each) cherry-flavored gelatin
1 can (12 ounces) cola
1 cup chopped pecans
1 package (8 ounces) cream cheese, cut into ¼-inch cubes (see Note)

In a medium-sized saucepan, bring the reserved pineapple syrup and cherry syrup to a boil over medium-high heat. Remove from the heat and add the gelatin, stirring until dissolved. Pour into a medium-sized bowl, add the cola, and chill for 1 hour, or until it starts to thicken. Stir in the pineapple, cherries, pecans, and cream cheese and spoon into a medium-sized bowl or gelatin mold. Chill for 3 hours, or until set. When ready to serve, if using a mold, dip the bottom of the mold in warm water for a few seconds, then invert onto a serving plate larger than the mold. Shake gently to loosen from the mold.

Note: The cream cheese should be cut into small chunks so it floats in the gelatin mixture instead of blending into it.

Fruity Cranberry Salad

6 to 9 servings

Don't save this one just for serving with the holiday turkey. It's bursting with fruity flavor!

2 packages (4 servings each) cherry-flavored gelatin
1 cup boiling water
1 container (12 ounces) cranberry-orange relish

1 can (20 ounces) crushed pineapple in heavy syrup, undrained
1 cup finely chopped pecans

In an 8-inch square baking dish, dissolve the gelatin in the boiling water. Add the remaining ingredients; mix well. Cover and chill for at least 4 hours, or until set.

Mandarin Orange Salad

How cool and refreshing! It's a colorful side dish to brighten up a porch luncheon, and it's a light low-fat dessert for anytime, anywhere.

1 container (16 ounces) cottage cheese

1 package (4-serving size) orange-flavored gelatin

1 can (11 ounces) mandarin oranges, drained

1 can (8 ounces) crushed pineapple, drained

1 container (8 ounces) frozen whipped topping, thawed

In a large bowl, combine the cottage cheese and gelatin; mix until well combined. Add the remaining ingredients; mix well. Spoon into a serving bowl, cover, and chill for at least 1 hour before serving.

Chilled Beet Salad

6 to 9 servings

Let's really wake up ho-hum beets by making a salad that's popular not only in the South, but everywhere!

1 can (20 ounces) crushed
   pineapple in heavy syrup,
   undrained
1 package (4-serving size)
   strawberry-flavored gelatin
1 can (8¼ ounces) sliced
   beets, drained and finely
   chopped, ⅓ cup liquid
   reserved

3 tablespoons white vinegar
1 teaspoon prepared
   horseradish
2 stalks celery, finely
   chopped

In a medium-sized saucepan, combine the pineapple with its syrup and the gelatin; bring to a boil over medium heat, stirring constantly. Add the remaining ingredients; mix well. Pour into an 8-inch square baking dish and chill for at least 4 hours, or until set. Serve, or cover and chill until ready to serve.

The Party Platter

Party and Finger Foods

continued

Mango Chutney Spread

about 2 cups

Chutney is simply a relish that's served as an accompaniment to meats and curried dishes. Now this one's extra-special 'cause it's made into a creamy spread—so it's a perfect predinner snack with crackers or thin slices of French bread, too!

1 package (8 ounces) cream cheese, softened
2 teaspoons curry powder
1 teaspoon Worcestershire sauce
¼ teaspoon hot pepper sauce
½ teaspoon salt
1 jar (9 ounces) mango chutney
1 container (3 ounces) real bacon bits

In a small bowl, combine the cream cheese, curry, Worcestershire sauce, hot pepper sauce, and salt; mix well. Place the cream cheese mixture in a shallow serving dish. Spoon the mango chutney over the top and sprinkle with the bacon bits. Serve immediately, or cover and chill until ready to serve.

Note: I usually take this out of the fridge 30 minutes before serving so it'll soften up and be nice and spreadable.

Pimiento Cheese Ball

about 2 cups

You'll have a ball making this easy party snack. And there's no need to wait for a get-together to have one of these on hand!

2 cups (8 ounces) shredded sharp Cheddar cheese
1 package (8 ounces) cream cheese, softened
1 jar (4 ounces) processed pimiento cheese spread
1 garlic clove, minced
¼ cup finely chopped pecans

In a large bowl, with an electric beater on medium speed, beat the Cheddar cheese, cream cheese, pimiento cheese, and garlic for 2 minutes, or until smooth. Place the mixture on waxed paper and form into a ball. Wrap in the waxed paper and chill for about 2 hours, or until firm. Place the pecans in a shallow dish. Remove the waxed paper from the cheese ball and roll it in the pecans, completely coating it. Serve, or wrap well and chill until ready to serve.

Note: No last-minute work for me, 'cause this can be made up to 3 days in advance!

Pineapple Sandwich Spread

about 3 cups

This is a sure winner when teamed with smoked ham or roast pork, but it's got a nice fresh taste that'll liven up almost any sandwich.

1 can (20 ounces) crushed pineapple in heavy syrup, drained, syrup reserved	2 eggs 1 tablespoon cornstarch ½ cup mayonnaise

In a small saucepan, whisk together the reserved pineapple juice, the eggs, and cornstarch. Place over medium heat and continue whisking for 3 to 4 minutes, or until the mixture thickens. Remove from the heat and allow to cool completely. Stir in the pineapple and mayonnaise. Transfer to a bowl, cover, and chill for at least 1 hour before serving.

Note: If not using this immediately, transfer it to an airtight container and store in the refrigerator; it should keep for up to 2 weeks. And besides using it as a sandwich spread, try it on crackers, or even as a stuffing for celery stalks.

Cheesy Ham Roll-ups

about 3 dozen

Talk about melt-in-your-mouth goodness. . . . Mmm, mmm! These go down so easy, you'd better make plenty—'cause they disappear practically as soon as they hit the table!

1 package (8 ounces) cream
   cheese, softened
2 tablespoons finely chopped
   fresh parsley

¼ teaspoon garlic powder
8 slices (8 ounces) deli ham

In a medium-sized bowl, combine the cream cheese, parsley, and garlic powder; mix well. Spread equally over the slices of ham. Roll up each slice tightly, jelly-roll style, starting from a short side. Cut each roll into 4 equal slices. Serve, or cover and chill until ready to serve.

Cola Meatballs

about 4 dozen

These super little cocktail meatballs get their rich flavor from a favorite soft drink!

1 pound ground beef
1 cup seasoned bread crumbs
2 tablespoons water
1 small onion, finely chopped, divided
1 teaspoon salt, divided
½ teaspoon black pepper, divided

1 garlic clove, minced
1 cup ketchup
1 cup cola
1 tablespoon Worcestershire sauce
½ of a medium-sized green bell pepper, finely chopped

Preheat the oven to 325°F. In a large bowl, combine the ground beef, bread crumbs, water, half of the onion, ½ teaspoon salt, and ¼ teaspoon black pepper; mix well. Form into 1-inch meatballs and place in a 9" × 13" baking dish. In a medium-sized bowl, combine the remaining ingredients, including the remaining onion, ½ teaspoon salt, and ¼ teaspoon black pepper; mix well. Pour the mixture over the meatballs and bake for 50 to 60 minutes, or until the meatballs are cooked through and the sauce is bubbling.

Spicy Hot Sausage Balls

about 5 dozen

Don't be fooled by the name—these are traditionally served instead of biscuits. They're little dough balls flavored with spicy sausage meat! And they're great dipped in mustard. Are you a dabber or a dunker?

1 package (16 ounces) hot
   pork sausage (see Note)
3 cups biscuit baking mix

1 cup (4 ounces) shredded
   sharp Cheddar cheese

Preheat the oven to 350°F. In a large bowl, combine all the ingredients. Using your hands, knead well until a soft dough forms. Roll the dough into 1-inch balls and place on a rimmed baking sheet. Bake for 12 to 15 minutes, or until the bottoms begin to brown and the sausage is no longer pink.

Note: Make sure to use a packaged hot sausage like Jimmy Dean® brand, not spicy Italian sausage from the meat counter—the consistency is different. Serve these with your favorite type of mustard or even ketchup as a dipping sauce.

Cheese Straws

about 10 dozen

Absolutely one of my favorites, these are easy to make and tasty as can be. And they're great for snack attacks, 'cause they're homemade-good and have no preservatives!

4 cups (16 ounces) shredded
   sharp Cheddar cheese
3 cups all-purpose flour
1 cup (2 sticks) butter,
   softened

1 teaspoon paprika
½ teaspoon salt
¼ teaspoon cayenne pepper

Preheat the oven to 400°F. In a large bowl, combine all the ingredients. Using your hands, knead well until a soft dough forms. Using a rolling pin, roll the dough out on a lightly floured surface to a ¼-inch thickness. Cut into ½" × 3" strips. Place on rimmed baking sheets that have been coated with nonstick cooking spray. Bake for 10 to 12 minutes, or until light golden. Serve warm, or allow to cool completely, then store in an airtight container until ready to use.

Golden Beef Roll-ups

about 1½ dozen

Bring some Southern warmth to a chilly winter party with these bite-sized treats. Y'all simply have to try 'em next time, y'hear?

1 package (8 ounces) refrigerated crescent rolls	½ teaspoon Worcestershire sauce
1 pound lean ground beef	1 teaspoon salt
1 small onion, chopped	¼ teaspoon black pepper

Preheat the oven to 400°F. Unroll the crescent dough and press the seams together to form one large rectangle of dough. In a medium-sized bowl, combine the remaining ingredients; mix well. Spread the beef mixture evenly over the dough. Roll up jelly-roll style, starting from a long side. Cut into ½-inch slices and place cut side down on a rimmed baking sheet that has been coated with nonstick cooking spray. Bake for 18 to 20 minutes, or until the beef is no longer pink and the crust is golden. Serve hot.

Note: Serve with Honey-Bacon Barbecue Sauce (page 126) or your other favorites for dipping.

Pickled Sausage Rolls

about 3½ dozen

I first had these years ago at a reception I attended in the Carolinas. I was on a road trip from New York to Florida. The only difference between those and mine is that the hostess made her dough from scratch. Honestly, I can't tell the difference with these!

1 package (7½ ounces)
  refrigerated biscuits
  (10 biscuits)

1 jar (4½ ounces) pickled
  sausage, well drained
  (see Note)

Preheat the oven to 425°F. Slightly flatten each biscuit and place a sausage in the center of each one. Fold the dough over the sausage and pinch the seams together. Cut each biscuit into 4 equal slices and place cut side down on large rimmed baking sheets that have been coated with nonstick cooking spray. Bake for 5 to 7 minutes, or until the biscuits are golden. Serve immediately.

Note: Pickled sausage can usually be found in the canned meat section of the supermarket near the deviled ham and Vienna sausages. Serve these with spicy brown mustard or your favorite dipping sauce.

Cheese Crisps

4 dozen

These are a cross between a cracker and a cookie, so maybe you should make a double batch. After all, it's not much more work, and it'll save you from starting all over after they eat up the first batch 1–2–3!

2 cups (8 ounces) shredded
   sharp Cheddar cheese
1½ cups self-rising flour
½ cup (1 stick) butter,
   softened

⅛ teaspoon cayenne pepper
48 pecan halves

In a large bowl, combine the cheese, flour, butter, and cayenne pepper until well mixed. Form into a 12-inch smooth log about 1½ inches in diameter. Wrap the log in waxed paper and freeze for 1 hour, or until thoroughly chilled. Preheat the oven to 250°F. Remove the waxed paper from the dough log and cut into ¼-inch slices. Press 1 pecan half onto the top of each slice. Place on a baking sheet that has been coated with nonstick cooking spray and bake for 40 to 45 minutes, or until the edges are golden and the crisps easily release from the pan.

Pepper Jelly Tarts

about 1½ dozen

Whether you're an old fan or a first-time taster of pepper jelly, you're gonna discover incredibly unique flavor with just one bite of these!

1 jar (5 ounces) processed
　cheese spread
½ cup (1 stick) butter,
　softened

1 cup all-purpose flour
1 tablespoon water
3 tablespoons pepper jelly

Preheat the oven to 375°F. In a medium-sized bowl, combine the cheese spread, butter, flour, and water; mix well. Roll the dough between 2 sheets of waxed paper to a ¼-inch thickness. Cut out circles with a 2-inch biscuit cutter and place ½ teaspoon pepper jelly in the center of each dough circle. Fold the dough over to form half-circles and pinch to seal the edges. Place on a large baking sheet and bake for 10 to 12 minutes, or until golden. Remove to a wire rack to cool completely. Store in an airtight container until ready to serve.

Note: If the dough becomes too soft to work with, freeze it for a few minutes till it firms up again. Check out the recipe on page 38 for making your own pepper jelly.

Snackin' Pecans

about 4 cups

Crunchy? Yes! Zippy? You bet! Always ready and waiting, too!

¼ cup (½ stick) butter
¼ cup Worcestershire sauce
2 teaspoons garlic powder

½ teaspoon salt
4 cups pecan halves

Preheat the oven to 375°F. In a large saucepan, combine the butter, Worcestershire sauce, garlic powder, and salt over medium heat. Cook for 2 to 3 minutes, or until the butter is melted, stirring frequently. Remove from the heat and stir in the pecans until thoroughly coated. Spread on a large rimmed cookie sheet and bake for 12 to 15 minutes, or until toasted. Remove to a paper towel–lined platter to drain and cool. Store in an airtight container until ready to serve.

Nutty Cheese Crackers

about 2 dozen

This is a lot of good tastes rolled into one, making great use of a Southern specialty: pecans!

2 cups (8 ounces) shredded
   sharp Cheddar cheese
1 cup self-rising flour
¾ cup finely chopped pecans

½ cup (1 stick) butter,
   softened
½ teaspoon salt
⅛ teaspoon cayenne pepper

In a medium-sized bowl, combine all the ingredients. Using your hands, knead well until a soft dough forms. Shape into an 8-inch log about 2 inches in diameter. Wrap tightly in plastic wrap and chill for about 30 minutes, until firm. Preheat the oven to 350°F. Unwrap and cut the log into ¼-inch slices. Place on a rimmed baking sheet that has been coated with nonstick cooking spray. Bake for 20 to 25 minutes, or until golden. Let stand for 5 minutes before removing from the baking sheet. Serve warm, or allow to cool completely, then store in an airtight container until ready to serve.

Rum Balls

about 4 dozen

Although rum has strong roots in the Caribbean, it has long been a part of Southern drinks, as well as desserts. Rum balls are a perfect, tasty example of why!

1 package (11 ounces) chocolate wafer cookies, crushed
1½ cups chopped pecans

½ cup light corn syrup
¼ cup light or dark rum
½ cup confectioners' sugar

In a large bowl, combine the crushed cookies and pecans; mix well. Stir in the corn syrup and rum until thoroughly combined. Place the confectioners' sugar in a shallow dish. Roll the cookie mixture into 1½-inch balls. Roll in the confectioners' sugar until completely coated. Serve, or store in an airtight container at room temperature until ready to serve.

Note: These tend to absorb most of the confectioners' sugar after coating, so be sure to coat them very heavily; you might even want to roll them in additional sugar just before serving.

Coconut Strawberries

about 5 dozen

What a great garnish for plates of finger sandwiches, or even for fancying up our cookie and other dessert trays!

1 can (14 ounces) sweetened condensed milk
1 package (14 ounces) shredded coconut
2 packages (4 servings each) strawberry-flavored gelatin
1 tablespoon sugar
1 teaspoon vanilla extract
2 tablespoons slivered almonds
⅛ teaspoon green food color

In a medium-sized bowl, combine the sweetened condensed milk, coconut, 1 package gelatin mix, the sugar, and vanilla; mix well. Pour the second package of gelatin into a shallow dish. Form the coconut mixture into 1-inch balls and roll in the gelatin until completely coated; set aside. In a small bowl, combine the slivered almonds and food color, tossing until the almonds turn green. Holding each coconut ball with the tips of your fingers, press a green almond into the top, forming a strawberry stem. Use your fingers to form each ball into the shape of a strawberry. Place on a baking sheet and allow to dry for at least 1 hour. Serve, or cover until ready to serve.

Note: For a great gift idea, save the plastic strawberry baskets from your strawberries. Fill the baskets with these, cover with plastic wrap (maybe even one of the pretty colored ones), and tie each one with a pretty ribbon.

Sugar-Glazed Pecans

about 1½ pounds

Isn't it nice to know that you're armed with a little nibble to serve with drinks? Wait till you hear comments like "Where did you buy these?" and "Would you share that recipe with me, *please*?"

2 tablespoons butter,
   softened
1 cup firmly packed light
   brown sugar

½ cup granulated sugar
½ cup sour cream
3 cups pecan halves

Coat a large rimmed baking sheet with the butter; set aside. In a large saucepan, combine the brown sugar, granulated sugar, and sour cream over medium-high heat; mix well. Cook for 8 to 10 minutes, stirring constantly; it's ready when a drop of the mixture forms a ball when dropped in cold water. Add the pecans and stir until thoroughly coated. Pour onto the baking sheet, separating the mixture into individual glazed pecan halves; work quickly so the mixture doesn't harden. Allow to cool, then serve, or store the cooled pecans in an airtight container until ready to serve.

Tangy Pickled Eggs

1 dozen

These are a real Southern specialty, and if you've never had the chance to try them, you'd better get ready to eat more than one!

12 eggs	4 teaspoons sugar
3 cups white vinegar	½ teaspoon salt
1 garlic clove, cut in half	½ teaspoon black pepper

Place the eggs in a large saucepan and add enough water to cover them. Bring to a boil over high heat. Remove from the heat, cover, and let sit for 20 minutes. Drain off the hot water and run cold water over the eggs. Let the eggs cool for 5 to 10 minutes, then drain and peel. Place in a large jar or bowl and set aside. In a large saucepan, combine the remaining ingredients and bring to a boil over high heat. Allow to cool slightly, then carefully pour the mixture over the eggs. Cover and chill overnight before serving.

Note: Covered tightly, these should keep in the refrigerator for up to 1 month. And because you might want to use them to make the perfect deviled eggs, I don't bother coloring these pink, as traditional recipes do.

Boiled Peanuts

2 pounds

In Georgia, peanut farmers celebrate the harvest with peanut boils. These are large outdoor get-togethers where everybody eats freshly boiled peanuts. Boy, are they good! They have a different taste from the roasted peanuts most of us are used to, so be prepared for a whole new treat!

6 cups water   1½ teaspoons salt
2 pounds green peanuts
   (see Note)

In a large pot, bring all the ingredients to a boil over high heat. Cover loosely and continue to boil for 2 hours, or until the peanut hulls open easily when pressed and the peanuts inside are soft. Drain and serve warm, or transfer to an airtight container and chill until ready to serve.

Note: It used to be that this could be made only when fresh green peanuts were in season. But today many supermarkets sell them frozen. The quantity of salt is really up to you, depending on how salty you like these.

Vegetable Spread Triangles

4 dozen

Whether these are served at a reception with a refreshing fruity punch or with a tall glass of iced tea, you know they'll be the talk of the get-together!

2 medium-sized carrots, grated
1 medium-sized cucumber, peeled, grated, and drained well
1 small onion, grated
1 package (8 ounces) cream cheese, softened
¼ cup mayonnaise
1 teaspoon salt
¼ teaspoon cayenne pepper
Six 6-inch pita breads

Preheat the broiler. In a medium-sized bowl, combine all the ingredients except the pita bread; mix well. Spread the cream cheese mixture evenly over the top of the pita breads and place on rimmed baking sheets. Broil the sandwiches for 2 to 3 minutes, or until heated through. Remove from the broiler and cut each pita into 8 wedges. Serve warm.

Pimiento Cheese Sandwiches

32 finger sandwiches

Mix it, spread it, cut it, and you're ready for any kind of drop-in company!

2 cups (8 ounces) finely
   shredded sharp Cheddar
   cheese
1 jar (7 ounces) diced
   pimientos, drained

½ cup mayonnaise
16 slices white bread

In a medium-sized bowl, combine all the ingredients except the bread; mix well. Spread the mixture evenly over 8 bread slices. Top with the remaining 8 bread slices, then cut into squares or triangles and serve.

Note: If you'd like, serve these hot. Just bake on a rimmed baking sheet in a 350°F. oven for 5 to 8 minutes, or until the bread is toasted and the cheese is melted. Then cut into squares or triangles.

Egg and Olive Sandwich Strips

15 sandwich strips

My dad used to love egg and olive sandwiches, and so do I! Whoever knew that by adding a few pecans, I'd be eating a favorite of the South!

2 hard-boiled eggs, finely chopped
1 jar (5 ounces) sliced pimiento-stuffed green olives, drained and finely chopped
1 small onion, finely chopped
1 cup finely chopped pecans
1 cup mayonnaise
10 slices whole wheat bread

In a large bowl, combine all the ingredients except the bread; mix well. Spread evenly onto 5 bread slices. Top with the remaining 5 bread slices. Cut the crusts from the sandwiches and cut each sandwich into 3 strips. Serve, or cover and chill until ready to serve.

Note: These can also be made on rye or pumpernickel bread, or even a combination, using one type of bread for the top and another for the bottom of each sandwich.

Peach Canapés

Be untraditional and serve these with a morning cup of coffee for a light beginning to the day!

1 package (8 ounces) cream
   cheese, softened
¾ cup peach preserves
½ cup chopped pecans,
   toasted (see Note)

½ teaspoon ground ginger
10 slices white bread

In a large bowl, combine the cream cheese, preserves, pecans, and ginger; mix well. Spread an equal amount of the mixture evenly over each bread slice and cut each into 4 squares.

Note: To toast the pecans, spread them in a single layer on a large rimmed baking sheet and bake at 425°F. for 7 to 9 minutes, or until golden. (Keep an eye on them, 'cause they may be ready sooner!) You can make up the cream cheese spread and keep it in the fridge, then spread it on bread for breakfast; it's great for unexpected company, too!

Apple-Cinnamon Finger Sandwiches

4 dozen

Platter these up with two or three other kinds of finger sandwiches, and let the party begin! Boy, I love parties!

1 package (8 ounces) cream cheese, softened	¼ teaspoon ground cinnamon
¼ cup apple butter	12 slices cinnamon-raisin bread
1 tablespoon mayonnaise	

In a medium-sized bowl, combine the cream cheese, apple butter, mayonnaise, and cinnamon; mix until smooth. Spread equal amounts of the mixture evenly over the bread slices. Cut into squares and serve immediately, or cover and chill until ready to serve.

Note: For an added touch of sweetness, sprinkle the tops of the squares with a mixture of cinnamon and sugar just before serving.

Barbecue

Outside Taste Made Inside Easy

NOTE: When using sauces or marinades for basting, baste food only up until the last 10 minutes of cooking, then bring the sauce or marinade to a boil for a few minutes before using on cooked foods. Otherwise, discard any remaining sauce or marinade that has come in contact with the uncooked or partially cooked meat or poultry or its juices.

Stovetop Barbecued Roast

6 to 8 servings

Traditionally, this roast was cooked in a big cast-iron pot over a wood fire. Obviously, things have changed—the pot can be your favorite one and the fire is a stovetop burner. But the taste . . . luckily, that rich barbecue taste hasn't changed much!

2 tablespoons butter
One 3-pound beef top or
   bottom round roast
1½ teaspoons salt
1 teaspoon black pepper
3 medium-sized onions,
   sliced
1 garlic clove, chopped

1 can (8 ounces) tomato
   sauce
¼ cup barbecue sauce
Juice of 1 lemon
2 tablespoons light brown
   sugar
½ teaspoon dry mustard

In a large pot, melt the butter over medium-high heat. Season the roast with the salt and pepper and cook for 5 to 7 minutes, turning to brown on all sides. Stir in the remaining ingredients until well mixed. Reduce the heat to low, cover, and simmer for 2¾ to 3 hours, or until the roast is fork-tender. Transfer the roast to a cutting board and slice. Return the slices to the pot and cook in the sauce for 3 to 5 minutes, or until heated through.

Peanut Flank Steak

4 to 5 servings

With peanuts so abundant in the South, it's no wonder the folks in Virginia and Georgia add a nutty flavor to so many of their recipes—yes, even steak!

1 cup chunky peanut butter
1 cup dry red wine
¼ cup (½ stick) butter,
   melted

1 garlic clove, minced
1 teaspoon cayenne pepper
1 teaspoon salt
One 2-pound beef flank steak

In a medium-sized bowl, combine all the ingredients except the steak; whisk until well combined. Place in a large resealable plastic storage bag and add the steak. Seal tightly and allow to marinate in the refrigerator for 2 hours. Preheat the broiler and place the steak on a broiler pan or rimmed baking sheet; reserve the marinade. Broil for 4 to 5 minutes per side for medium, or until desired doneness, basting several times with the marinade until the last 5 minutes of broiling. Discard any remaining marinade. Slice the steak and serve.

Note: Thinly sliced and placed on hoagie rolls, this makes great sandwiches.

Southern-Style Brisket

6 to 8 servings

A few minutes to put this together, then into the oven it goes so the oven can do the rest of the work. What do you know—you get to be a guest at dinner, too!

½ cup barbecue sauce
½ cup ketchup
½ cup apple cider vinegar
½ cup firmly packed light brown sugar

⅓ cup water
1 envelope (1 ounce) onion soup mix
One 4- to 5-pound beef brisket

Preheat the oven to 350°F. In a medium-sized bowl, combine all the ingredients except the brisket; mix well. Place the brisket in a roasting pan that has been coated with nonstick cooking spray. Pour the barbecue sauce mixture over the brisket and cover tightly with aluminum foil. Bake for 3 to 3½ hours, or until fork-tender. Slice across the grain and serve with the sauce from the pan.

Barbecued Short Ribs

4 to 6 servings

Ask any Texan about true barbecue, and he'll insist that it be made with beef, not pork. You only have to taste this recipe to know why!

4 pounds beef short ribs
1 small onion, chopped
1 cup ketchup
½ cup water
¼ cup Worcestershire sauce

¼ cup firmly packed light
    brown sugar
2 teaspoons prepared yellow
    mustard
1 teaspoon salt

In a large pot, bring all the ingredients to a boil over high heat, stirring until well mixed. Reduce the heat to low, cover, and cook for 2½ to 3 hours, or until the short ribs are tender, stirring occasionally.

Note: I cook these even longer because I like the meat to be falling off the bones.

Smothered Pork Chops

4 servings

The gang'll go hog-wild over these yummy chops smothered in rich chili sauce!

4 pork loin chops (1½ to 2 pounds total), 1 inch thick	3 tablespoons light brown sugar
1 teaspoon salt	1 tablespoon chopped onion
¼ teaspoon black pepper	1 teaspoon Worcestershire sauce
1 cup chili sauce	1 teaspoon dry mustard
¼ cup white vinegar	

Preheat the oven to 350°F. Season the pork chops with the salt and pepper and place in a 9" × 13" baking dish that has been coated with nonstick cooking spray. In a medium-sized bowl, combine the remaining ingredients; mix well and pour over the pork chops. Bake for 40 to 45 minutes for medium, or until desired doneness beyond that. Serve with the sauce spooned over the pork chops.

Low Country Ribs

If you followed the unbelievably aromatic smoke to Savannah or Charleston, it would lead you to a barbecue like you've never seen. Boy, do they serve up lots of good barbecue there, just like this. Oh—right before you take these ribs off the grill, slather them with your favorite barbecue sauce. Mmm, mmm . . . it's lip-smackin' good!

½ cup water
½ cup white vinegar
¼ cup vegetable oil

¼ cup sugar
5 to 6 pounds country-style
   pork ribs

Preheat the oven to 350°F. In a small bowl, combine the water, vinegar, oil, and sugar; mix well. Place the ribs in a 9" × 13" baking dish that has been coated with nonstick cooking spray. Pour the vinegar mixture over the ribs and bake for 1¾ to 2 hours, or until the ribs are tender. Remove from the liquid and cut into individual ribs.

Note: Top these with Sweet Barbecue Sauce (page 122), or any of your favorite barbecue sauces.

Country-Glazed Spareribs

These ribs are smothered in a sweet and tangy sauce that's simply mouthwatering and rib-ticklin' good!

½ teaspoon garlic powder
1 teaspoon salt
½ teaspoon black pepper
4 to 5 pounds pork spareribs
2 onions, sliced

1 cup water
1 cup tomato juice
½ cup apple jelly
¼ cup soy sauce
¼ cup white vinegar

Preheat the oven to 350°F. In a small bowl, combine the garlic powder, salt, and pepper. Season the ribs with the mixture and place in a roasting pan that has been lined with aluminum foil and coated with nonstick cooking spray. Place the onion slices over the ribs and add the water to the pan. Cover tightly with aluminum foil and bake for 1½ hours. Drain off any excess liquid. In a medium-sized bowl, combine the remaining ingredients; mix well. Pour over the ribs and bake, uncovered, for 50 to 60 minutes more, or until the ribs are tender, basting every 15 minutes. Cut into individual ribs and serve.

Skillet Barbecued Chicken

When we crave the taste of barbecue but the weather isn't cooperating, we can grab a skillet and let the inside stovetop barbecue begin!

¼ cup (½ stick) butter
1 small onion, chopped
1 garlic clove, minced
One 3- to 3½-pound chicken, cut into 8 pieces
½ teaspoon salt
¼ cup steak sauce

¼ cup tomato sauce
¼ cup firmly packed light brown sugar
2 tablespoons Worcestershire sauce
1 teaspoon hot pepper sauce
¼ teaspoon chili powder

In a large deep skillet, melt the butter over medium heat and sauté the onion and garlic for 5 to 7 minutes, or until the onion is tender. Season the chicken with the salt, then add it to the skillet and cook for 8 to 10 minutes, turning to brown on all sides. Meanwhile, in a medium-sized bowl, combine the remaining ingredients; mix well. Add to the chicken, cover, and cook for 35 to 40 minutes, or until no pink remains in the chicken and the juices run clear, stirring occasionally.

Peach-Glazed Chicken

4 servings

This recipe was adapted from a Georgia-style barbecued chicken with peach sauce. I'll tell you what, instead of the authentic version where you have to dig a pit to slow-roast your chickens, I decided to make this skillet-style. I know you'll be happy I made that change!

¼ cup all-purpose flour
4 boneless, skinless chicken breast halves (1 to 1½ pounds total)
2 tablespoons butter
1 package (20 ounces) frozen sliced peaches
1½ cups firmly packed light brown sugar
2 celery stalks, finely chopped
1 small onion, chopped
½ of a medium-sized red bell pepper, chopped
2 tablespoons lemon juice
¾ teaspoon cayenne pepper
½ teaspoon salt

Place the flour in a shallow dish. Dip the chicken breasts in the flour, coating completely. In a large skillet, melt the butter over medium-high heat. Add the coated chicken and brown for 2 to 3 minutes per side. Transfer the chicken to a platter and set aside. Add the remaining ingredients to the skillet and cook for 4 to 5 minutes, or until the peaches are thawed and the sauce begins to thicken. Return the chicken to the skillet and cook for 8 to 10 minutes, or until no pink remains in the chicken and the sauce has thickened.

Note: To enjoy every last bit of the peach sauce, serve this over hot cooked rice.

Barbecue Chip Chicken

4 servings

A perfect marriage—two of our favorites together in one yummy dish. Sure, it's a little untraditional, but who said marriage has to be traditional?!

½ cup ranch salad dressing
1 teaspoon garlic powder
¼ teaspoon cayenne pepper
1 bag (6 ounces) barbecue-
   flavored potato chips,
   crushed

4 boneless, skinless chicken
   breast halves (1 to 1½
   pounds total)

Preheat the oven to 400°F. In a shallow bowl, combine the dressing, garlic powder, and cayenne pepper; mix well. Place the crushed potato chips in another shallow bowl. Dip the chicken into the dressing mixture, then into the crushed potato chips, coating completely. Place on a rimmed baking sheet that has been coated with nonstick cooking spray. Bake for 15 to 20 minutes, or until no pink remains in the chicken.

Note: Before dipping, you may want to cut the chicken into long strips to form chicken fingers. If you'd like, serve with additional ranch dressing for dipping.

Sweet Mustard Barbecued Chicken

4 to 6 servings

North Carolinians sure are proud of their barbecue, and this sweet mustard sauce is certainly something to be proud of. Whether it's served on chicken or pork, it's a taste you're gonna love!

One 3- to 3½-pound chicken, cut into 8 pieces
½ cup dark corn syrup
½ cup ketchup
½ cup prepared yellow mustard
¼ cup white vinegar

Preheat the oven to 350°F. Place the chicken pieces on a large rimmed baking sheet that has been coated with nonstick cooking spray. Bake for 30 to 40 minutes. Preheat the grill to medium heat. In a medium-sized saucepan, combine the corn syrup, ketchup, mustard, and vinegar and cook over medium heat until heated through. Brush the mixture over the chicken and grill for 5 minutes. Turn the chicken, brush again with the mixture, and grill for another 5 minutes, or until no pink remains in the chicken and the juices run clear.

Note: Make sure your fire isn't too hot, because you don't want the outside of the chicken to get overdone before the rest of it's cooked through.

Sweet Barbecue Sauce

about 1½ cups

This savory homemade version of barbecue sauce will have you tossing out the bottled ones, for sure!

1 cup ketchup
¼ cup lemon juice
¼ cup (½ stick) butter
¼ cup firmly packed dark
  brown sugar
1 small onion, finely
  chopped

1 garlic clove, minced
2 tablespoons prepared
  yellow mustard
2 tablespoons Worcestershire
  sauce

In a large saucepan, combine all the ingredients over medium heat. Bring to a boil and allow to boil for 15 minutes, or until the sauce has thickened and the onion is tender, stirring frequently. Serve warm.

Note: This is great for basting or dipping!

Birmingham-Style White Sauce

about 3 cups

This poultry barbecue sauce, which originated in Birmingham, Alabama, is a zippy alternative to traditional red barbecue sauce.

2 cups mayonnaise
¼ cup white vinegar
¼ cup lemon juice
1 tablespoon Worcestershire
    sauce

2 tablespoons sugar
2 tablespoons black pepper

In a medium-sized bowl, combine all the ingredients; mix well. Serve, or cover and chill until ready to use.

Note: I like to serve this over roasted or smoked chicken and turkey, but it goes well with pork, too.

North Carolina Barbecue Sauce

about 1⅔ cups

I love North Carolina–style barbecue sauces 'cause they all seem to get an extra kick from mustard. Mmm!

1 cup apple cider vinegar
⅔ cup prepared yellow
  mustard
½ cup firmly packed light
  brown sugar

2 tablespoons butter
1 teaspoon soy sauce
1 teaspoon chili powder
¼ teaspoon cayenne pepper
1 teaspoon black pepper

In a medium-sized saucepan, combine all the ingredients over medium heat. Bring to a boil and allow to boil for 5 minutes, or until the sauce has thickened, stirring constantly. Serve warm.

Note: This is a super sauce that's good for basting or as a warm dipping sauce.

Lemon Barbecue Marinade

about 3/4 cup

As we travel the South, every state—practically every city—claims to have its own variation on a barbecue marinade/basting sauce. They're all so good! I can't put my finger on exactly where this variation of a lemon-based sauce comes from, but it sure is tasty with pork and beef.

½ cup vegetable oil
⅓ cup lemon juice
1 tablespoon grated onion
1 garlic clove, minced

¼ teaspoon hot pepper sauce
¼ teaspoon dried thyme
⅛ teaspoon dried marjoram
1 teaspoon salt

In a small bowl, whisk all the ingredients together until well blended. Use as a marinade for your favorite fish or poultry: Allow it to marinate for at least 30 minutes, then bake, broil, grill, or barbecue as desired, reserving the excess marinade. Meanwhile, in a small saucepan, bring the marinade to a boil. Let boil for 10 minutes, then serve as a sauce over the fish or poultry.

Note: You can always add more hot pepper sauce if you want it spicy.

Honey-Bacon Barbecue Sauce

about 3½ cups

Thank goodness all barbecue sauces are not created equal! This one keeps the grilling far from boring.

½ pound bacon, chopped
1 medium-sized onion, diced
1 garlic clove, minced
1 can (14½ ounces) ready-to-use chicken broth
1 bottle (12 ounces) chili sauce

1 cup honey
2 tablespoons lemon juice
1 teaspoon hot pepper sauce
1 teaspoon salt
½ teaspoon black pepper

In a large pot, cook the bacon for 5 to 6 minutes over medium-high heat, or until lightly browned, stirring occasionally. Add the onion and garlic and cook for 2 to 3 minutes, or until the onion is tender, stirring constantly. Add the remaining ingredients and bring to a boil. Reduce the heat to medium-low and cook for 40 to 45 minutes, or until the sauce has thickened, stirring occasionally. Serve warm.

Lip-Smackin' Barbecue Sauce

about 1½ cups

You'll be the apple of their eyes when you serve up this lip-smackin' cider vinegar–based sauce that's popular throughout the Carolinas and Alabama.

1 cup apple cider vinegar
1 cup ketchup
¼ cup water
2 teaspoons prepared yellow
   mustard
1 teaspoon Worcestershire
   sauce

1 teaspoon chili powder
¼ teaspoon cayenne pepper
½ teaspoon salt
2 teaspoons black pepper

In a large saucepan, combine all the ingredients over medium heat. Bring to a boil and allow to boil for 15 to 20 minutes, or until slightly thickened, stirring frequently. Serve warm.

Bourbon Barbecue Sauce

about 1¼ cups

When you're driving down South and pass the "Welcome to Tennessee" sign, you'll find that bourbon is no stranger to the kitchen or to the barbecue.

1 small onion, finely
   chopped
½ cup Dijon-style mustard
½ cup firmly packed dark
   brown sugar

¼ cup bourbon
2 teaspoons Worcestershire
   sauce
½ teaspoon salt

In a medium-sized saucepan, bring all the ingredients to a boil over medium heat. Reduce the heat to low and cook for 15 to 18 minutes, or until the sauce has thickened and the onion is tender, stirring frequently. Serve warm.

The Meat Case

Main-Dish Meats

continued

Country-Fried Steak

4 servings

Whatever you do, don't clean out this skillet after you brown up the steaks! The pan drippings make the gravy, and that makes the whole dish.

4 beef cubed steaks (1 to 1¼
    pounds total), pounded to
    ¼-inch thickness
1 teaspoon salt, divided
½ teaspoon black pepper,
    divided

¾ cup buttermilk
¾ cup plus 3 tablespoons all-
    purpose flour, divided
½ cup vegetable shortening
1½ cups milk

Season the steaks with ½ teaspoon salt and ¼ teaspoon pepper; set aside. Place the buttermilk in a shallow dish. Place ¾ cup flour in another shallow dish. Dip the steaks in the buttermilk, then in the flour, coating completely. In a large deep skillet, heat the shortening over medium-high heat until hot but not smoking. Add the steaks and cook for 3 to 4 minutes per side, or until cooked through and the coating is golden. Drain on a paper towel–lined platter and cover to keep warm. Add the remaining 3 tablespoons flour, ½ teaspoon salt, and ¼ tea-spoon pepper to the skillet. Cook for 2 to 3 minutes, or until the flour is browned, stirring constantly. Add the milk and stir until the gravy thickens. Serve the steaks topped with the gravy.

Cola Roast

Pop open a can of this favorite beverage, and you've got the start of a favorite main dish!

¼ cup all-purpose flour
One 3- to 4-pound beef
    chuck roast, trimmed
¼ cup vegetable oil
1 can (14½ ounces) diced
    tomatoes, undrained
1 can (12 ounces) cola

1 medium-sized onion, finely
    chopped
2 garlic cloves, minced
1 package (1¼ ounces) dry
    spaghetti sauce mix
½ teaspoon black pepper

Place the flour in a large bowl. Add the roast and roll to coat all sides with the flour. In a large pot, heat the oil over medium-high heat until hot but not smoking. Add the roast and any remaining flour to the pot and cook for 6 to 8 minutes, turning to brown on all sides. Add the remaining ingredients to the pot; mix well and bring to a boil. Reduce the heat to medium, cover, and cook for 1½ to 2 hours, or until the roast is just tender, stirring occasionally. Uncover and cook for 20 to 30 more minutes, or until the gravy has thickened. Remove the roast to a cutting board and slice. Serve topped with the gravy.

Salt-Crusted Beef

As this cooks, the salt forms a crust around the meat, keeping it nice and moist. We end up with a juicy, flavorful roast. And no, the salt crust doesn't make the meat too salty!

⅓ cup vegetable oil	One 2½- to 3-pound beef eye
1 small onion, finely	of the round roast,
chopped	trimmed
2 garlic cloves, minced	4 cups kosher (coarse) salt
½ teaspoon black pepper	1 cup water

In a large resealable plastic storage bag, combine the oil, onion, garlic, and pepper; close tightly and shake to mix well. Place the roast in the bag, seal, and coat it completely with the oil mixture. Marinate in the refrigerator for 2 hours. Preheat the oven to 350°F. Line a roasting pan with aluminum foil. In a medium-sized bowl, combine the salt and water; mix well. Place half of the salt mixture in the center of the lined pan. Place the roast on the salt mixture, then coat with the remaining salt mixture, completely coating the roast and forming a crust about ½ inch thick. Bake for 55 minutes for medium doneness, or until desired doneness beyond that. Remove from the oven, tap the salt crust with the back of a knife, remove, and discard. Slice and serve.

Beef Stroganoff

4 to 6 servings

How about a change of pace one night this week? This is one of those recipes we can't wait to make once we remember just how good it is.

¼ cup (½ stick) butter
1½ pounds boneless beef top sirloin steak, cut into ¼-inch strips
1 small onion, finely chopped
1 garlic clove, minced
2 tablespoons all-purpose flour
½ teaspoon black pepper

1 can (10¾ ounces) condensed cream of mushroom soup
1 can (10¾ ounces) condensed cream of chicken soup
¼ pound fresh mushrooms, sliced
1 cup sour cream

In a large skillet, melt the butter over medium heat. Add the steak strips, onion, and garlic and cook for 5 to 7 minutes, until the steak is no longer pink, stirring frequently. Add the flour and pepper; mix well. Add the soups and mushrooms; mix well. Reduce the heat to low and simmer for 8 to 10 minutes, or until the beef is tender. Stir in the sour cream and cook for 2 to 4 minutes, or until the mixture is heated through. Serve immediately.

Note: For a complete stroganoff dinner, serve this over hot cooked egg noodles.

Old-fashioned Beef Pot Roast

4 to 6 servings

It seems as if some version of pot roast is popular in just about every culture and in every type of regional cooking. Nothing beats the perfection of an old-fashioned recipe!

½ cup all-purpose flour
1 teaspoon salt
½ teaspoon black pepper
One 3- to 4-pound beef
   bottom round roast,
   trimmed

¼ cup vegetable oil
4 cups water

In a large bowl, combine the flour, salt, and pepper; mix well. Rinse the beef and place in the flour mixture while still wet, turning to coat completely. In a large pot, heat the oil over medium heat until hot but not smoking. Add the coated beef and cook for 5 to 6 minutes, turning to brown on all sides. Add the water and bring to a boil. Cover and cook for 1½ to 1¾ hours, or until the beef is fork-tender and the sauce has thickened.

Note: If the cover to your pot has a vent, then allow it to vent; otherwise, use a toothpick to keep the cover slightly ajar, allowing a little steam to escape during the cooking.

Bourbon Steaks

4 servings

The South is certainly well known for its bourbon, and when it's used as the highlight flavor on thick juicy steaks . . . watch out!

½ cup honey
½ cup molasses
½ cup bourbon
2 garlic cloves, minced
1 tablespoon ground ginger

1 teaspoon crushed red
   pepper
4 boneless beef loin strip
   steaks (8 ounces each)

In a medium-sized bowl, combine all the ingredients except the steaks; mix well. Place the steaks in a 9" × 13" baking dish and pour the marinade over the top. Cover and chill for 1 hour. Preheat the broiler. Remove the steaks from the marinade and place on a broiler pan, reserving the marinade. Broil for 6 to 8 minutes per side for medium, or until desired doneness. Meanwhile, in a medium-sized saucepan, bring the reserved marinade to a boil over medium-high heat. Let boil for 3 to 5 minutes, or until the sauce thickens. Pour the sauce over the steaks just before serving.

Sauerbraten with Gingersnap Gravy

4 servings

Sounds German, huh? This seemed to turn up over and over in my conversations with people from all over the South. Originally Southern or not, it's served there a lot now . . . and it's really tasty!

3 tablespoons butter
4 beef cubed steaks
   (1 to 1½ pounds total)
1 small onion, finely
   chopped
½ teaspoon salt
½ teaspoon black pepper
1 jar (12 ounces) brown gravy

1 tablespoon white vinegar
¼ cup water
½ cup coarsely crushed
   gingersnap cookies
1 tablespoon light brown
   sugar
½ cup sour cream

In a large skillet, melt the butter over medium-high heat. Add the cubed steaks, onion, salt, and pepper and cook for 6 to 8 minutes, or until the steaks are browned on both sides. Stir in the gravy, vinegar, water, cookie crumbs, and brown sugar and bring to a boil. Reduce the heat to low, cover, and simmer for 25 to 30 minutes, or until the steak is tender. Stir in the sour cream and cook for 3 to 4 minutes, or until well blended and heated through. Serve immediately.

Family Reunion Brisket

6 to 8 servings

In the South there are just as many reasons to get the whole gang together as there are yummy dishes to enjoy! Here's one that goes a long way with a crowd.

8 cups water
2 large onions, quartered
1 cinnamon stick
½ teaspoon whole cloves
1 teaspoon salt
One 4- to 5-pound beef
 brisket

1½ cups firmly packed light
 brown sugar
½ cup apple juice
⅓ cup prepared yellow
 mustard

In a large pot, combine the water, onions, cinnamon stick, cloves, and salt over high heat. Add the brisket and bring to a boil. Reduce the heat to medium, cover, and cook for 2 to 2½ hours, or until the brisket is fork-tender. Preheat the broiler. Remove the brisket from the pot and place in a roasting pan that has been lined with aluminum foil and coated with non-stick cooking spray. In a medium-sized bowl, combine the brown sugar, apple juice, and mustard; mix well. Coat the brisket with the brown sugar mixture and broil for 3 to 5 minutes, or until the sugar melts and the mixture is bubbly. Slice across the grain and serve with the sauce from the pan.

Down-home Meat Loaf

6 to 8 servings

Meat loaf is an easy put-together dish, and it always seems to adapt well to added flavorings. This one is a perfect example!

1½ pounds ground beef
⅔ cup plain dry bread
   crumbs (see Note)
1 cup milk
2 eggs
1 small onion, finely
   chopped
⅛ teaspoon rubbed sage

1 teaspoon salt
⅛ teaspoon black pepper
¼ cup ketchup
3 tablespoons light brown
   sugar
1 teaspoon dry mustard
¼ teaspoon ground nutmeg

Preheat the oven to 350°F. In a large bowl, combine the ground beef, bread crumbs, milk, eggs, onion, sage, salt, and pepper; mix well. Place in a 9" × 5" loaf pan that has been coated with nonstick cooking spray. In a small bowl, combine the remaining ingredients and spread over the top of the meat mixture. Bake for 50 to 60 minutes, or until no pink remains in the meat. Allow to stand for 10 minutes, then slice and serve.

Note: This is a soft meat loaf; if you like yours a bit firmer, use 1 cup bread crumbs instead of ⅔ cup.

Stuffed Cabbage Bundles

6 to 8 servings

These little bundles are perfect for combining yesterday's flavors with today's shortcuts! Make 'em the night before, and you'll look forward to that home-cooked taste all day long!

1 medium-sized head
   cabbage, cored
5 cups water
1½ teaspoons salt, divided
1½ pounds ground beef
1 medium-sized green bell
   pepper, chopped
1 medium-sized onion,
   chopped

½ cup plain dry bread
   crumbs
½ cup chili sauce
¼ teaspoon black pepper
1 jar (12 ounces) beef gravy
½ cup sour cream
½ cup firmly packed light
   brown sugar

In a large pot, combine the head of cabbage, the water, and 1 teaspoon salt. Cover and bring to a boil over high heat. Allow to boil for 12 to 15 minutes, or until the cabbage is tender; drain and set aside. Preheat the oven to 350°F. In a large bowl, combine the ground beef, green pepper, onion, bread crumbs, chili sauce, the remaining ½ teaspoon salt, and the black pepper; mix well. Carefully remove 12 to 18 cabbage leaves, depending on size; reserve the remaining cabbage for another use. Divide the ground beef mixture equally among the cabbage leaves, placing it in the center of each leaf. Starting at the core end of the leaves, make rolls about 1" × 2½", folding over the sides and rolling loosely. Place the rolls seam side down in a 9" × 13" baking dish that has been coated with nonstick cooking spray. In a medium-sized bowl, combine the gravy, sour cream, and brown sugar; mix well. Pour the gravy mixture evenly over the cabbage rolls. Cover tightly with aluminum foil and bake for 1 hour. Remove the aluminum foil and bake for 10 to 15 more minutes, or until the beef is no longer pink and the cabbage is very tender. Allow to stand for 5 minutes, then serve.

Hamburger Meal in One

4 servings

If you don't like doing dishes, be sure to check out this recipe. Know why? It cooks in foil packets, it's served in foil pockets, and when it's time for cleanup, you just throw away the foil packets!

1 pound ground beef
½ cup crushed butter-
   flavored crackers
¼ cup chili sauce
2 large potatoes, thinly sliced
1 large onion, thinly sliced
1 medium-sized green bell
   pepper, cut into 1-inch
   chunks

½ teaspoon salt
¼ teaspoon black pepper
1 can (10¾ ounces)
   condensed cream of
   mushroom soup

Preheat the oven to 400°F. In a medium-sized bowl, combine the ground beef, cracker crumbs, and chili sauce; mix well. Form into 8 patties and set aside. Coat four 12" × 18" pieces of aluminum foil with nonstick cooking spray and top each one with equal amounts of the potatoes, onion, and green pepper. Sprinkle the salt and pepper evenly over the vegetables. Place 2 beef patties over each pile of vegetables and top each with an equal amount of the soup. Seal each foil packet and place on a large baking sheet. Bake for 40 to 45 minutes, or until the beef is no longer pink and the vegetables are tender.

Ground Beef Roll

6 to 8 servings

Dazzle the gang with this rolled meat loaf that oozes with cheese.

2 pounds lean ground beef
3 slices white bread, torn into small pieces
2 eggs
¼ cup prepared yellow mustard

1 teaspoon salt
⅛ teaspoon black pepper
2 cups (8 ounces) shredded sharp Cheddar cheese
¼ cup chopped fresh parsley
1 cup barbecue sauce

Preheat the oven to 400°F. In a medium-sized bowl, combine the ground beef, bread, eggs, mustard, salt, and pepper. Mix with your hands until well blended. Place on a 12" × 16" piece of waxed paper and firmly pat into a 10" × 12" rectangle. In a small bowl, combine the cheese and parsley; mix well. Sprinkle the cheese mixture evenly over the ground beef mixture. Roll up jelly-roll style, starting from a short end, by lifting with the waxed paper and peeling off the paper as you roll. Seal the seam well. Place seam side down in a 7" × 11" baking dish that has been coated with nonstick cooking spray. Pour the barbecue sauce over the roll and bake for 55 to 60 minutes, or until no pink remains in the beef. Remove from the oven and allow to stand for 10 minutes. Slice and serve.

Liver and Onions

Liver is one of those foods that people have a love/hate relationship with—either they love it or hate it! But the key to making good liver is soaking it in milk to mellow the strong taste. And then you have to be sure not to overcook it.

1 pound beef liver, cut into serving-sized pieces
1 cup milk
½ cup all-purpose flour
½ teaspoon salt
¼ teaspoon black pepper
½ cup vegetable oil
1 large onion, cut into ¼-inch slices
1½ cups water

In a small bowl, combine the liver and milk and allow to stand for 15 minutes. In a shallow dish, combine the flour, salt, and pepper. In a large skillet, heat the oil over medium-high heat until hot but not smoking. Add the onion and sauté for 3 to 4 minutes, or until the onion is tender. Meanwhile, remove the liver from the milk and dip it in the flour mixture, coating completely. Add the liver to the onions and cook for 3 to 4 minutes per side, or until browned. Reserve 3 tablespoons of the flour mixture. Remove the liver and onions from the skillet; set aside. Add the reserved 3 tablespoons flour mixture to the skillet and cook for 2 to 3 minutes, or until browned, stirring constantly. Add the water; mix well. Return the liver and onions to the skillet and cook for 4 to 5 minutes, or until heated through.

Hot Dogs with Chili Sauce

12 servings

Hot dog suppers are often held as big fund-raisers for churches in the South—especially in the Carolinas, Georgia, and Alabama. This is the version that shows up most often!

1 pound ground beef
1½ cups water
1 large onion, finely chopped
¼ cup ketchup
2 tablespoons chili powder
1 tablespoon prepared yellow
  mustard

½ teaspoon salt
½ teaspoon black pepper
12 hot dogs
12 hot dog rolls, split

In a large pot, combine the ground beef and water over high heat, stirring until the beef is crumbly. Add the onion, ketchup, chili powder, mustard, salt, and pepper. Bring to a boil, then reduce the heat to medium-high. Cook for 35 to 40 minutes, or until most of the liquid has evaporated, stirring occasionally. Cook the hot dogs in a pot of boiling water for 6 to 8 minutes, or until heated through. Place in the rolls and top with the chili sauce. Serve immediately.

Note: These are often served sprinkled with shredded cheese and additional chopped onion. Cook the hot dogs any way you like—I especially like to grill them before topping them with the chili sauce.

Southern-Fried Pork Chops

4 servings

This is a "must" in all Southern households. One bite will tell you why!

1 cup all-purpose flour
1 teaspoon salt
½ teaspoon black pepper
1 cup water

4 pork loin chops
  (1½ to 2 pounds total),
  1 inch thick
2 cups vegetable shortening

In a shallow dish, combine the flour, salt, and pepper. Place the water in another shallow dish. Dip the pork chops in the water, then in the flour mixture, coating completely. In a large deep skillet, heat the shortening over medium heat until hot but not smoking. Add the pork chops and cook for 7 to 8 minutes per side, or until cooked through and the coating is golden. Drain on a paper towel–lined platter. Serve immediately.

Note: The trick is to heat the shortening till it's hot but not burning. That way, you get a nice crispy outside without the pork chops becoming greasy.

Asian-Marinated Pork Chops

4 servings

The Asian part is the marinade, but these chops are still comfortably Southern!

½ cup soy sauce
½ cup lemon juice
2 tablespoons ground ginger
1 teaspoon minced garlic

4 pork loin chops
  (1½ to 2 pounds total),
  ¾ inch thick
3 tablespoons butter

In a small bowl, combine all the ingredients except the pork chops and butter; mix well. Place the chops in a 9" × 13" baking dish and pour the soy sauce mixture over the top, turning the pork chops to coat thoroughly. Cover and chill for 2 hours, turning after 1 hour. Remove the chops from the marinade and discard the marinade. In a large skillet, melt the butter over medium heat and cook the pork chops for 5 to 7 minutes per side, or until cooked through. Serve immediately.

Hominy Sausage Casserole

These ingredients team up for a great potluck dish!

1 package (16 ounces) hot pork sausage (see Note, page 149)

1 can (15½ ounces) white hominy, drained

1 can (15½ ounces) yellow hominy, drained

1½ cups (6 ounces) shredded sharp Cheddar cheese, divided

1 jar (2 ounces) chopped pimientos, drained

1 small onion, finely chopped

4 eggs

1 tablespoon chopped fresh parsley

Preheat the oven to 350°F. In a large bowl, combine the sausage, white and yellow hominy, ½ cup cheese, the pimientos, onion, eggs, and parsley; mix well. Spoon into an 8-inch square baking dish that has been coated with nonstick cooking spray. Sprinkle the remaining 1 cup cheese evenly over the top of the casserole. Bake for 50 to 55 minutes, or until the sausage is no longer pink and the cheese is golden. Cut and serve.

Skillet Sausage Gravy

4 to 6 servings

This is especially enjoyable on a chilly day. Smother flaky biscuits with it and you'll warm up your gang for sure!

2 tablespoons butter
1 package (16 ounces) hot
   pork sausage (see Note)
3 tablespoons all-purpose
   flour

1 tablespoon Worcestershire
   sauce
1½ cups milk

In a large skillet, melt the butter over medium-high heat and heat for 1 to 1½ minutes, or until browned. Add the sausage and cook for 6 to 8 minutes, or until no pink remains, stirring to crumble the sausage. Add the flour; mix well. Add the Worcestershire sauce and milk; mix well. Cook for 2 to 4 minutes, or until the gravy thickens, stirring constantly.

Note: Serve over biscuits with eggs and grits for a breakfast that will satisfy them every time. Make sure to use the hot pork sausage that comes in a tube, not hot Italian pork sausage from the meat case. That way you'll get a finer-textured gravy.

Baked Green Ham

No, this isn't a Dr. Seuss recipe! Green ham was what early Southern settlers called ham, or leg of pork, that was fresh, not cured.

One 15- to 17-pound fresh ham	1½ teaspoons salt
¾ teaspoon garlic powder	1½ teaspoons black pepper

Preheat the oven to 350°F. Place the ham skin side up in a roasting pan that has been lined with aluminum foil. In a small bowl, combine the garlic powder, salt, and pepper; mix well and rub over the entire surface of the ham. Bake for 4½ to 5 hours, or until a meat thermometer inserted in the center of the ham registers 170°F. The skin will brown and separate from the meat. Slice and serve.

Skillet Glazed Ham

4 to 6 servings

Ham was no stranger to the early Southern settlers. It was so popular 'cause, with little or no refrigeration, cured ham was a safe choice. Today we eat it just because of its super taste!

1 can (8¼ ounces) pineapple slices, drained, juice reserved
1 jar (6 ounces) maraschino cherries, drained, juice reserved

½ cup firmly packed light brown sugar
½ teaspoon whole cloves
2 tablespoons butter
One 2- to 2½-pound ham steak

In a small bowl, combine the reserved pineapple and cherry juices, the brown sugar, and cloves; mix well and set aside. In a large skillet, melt the butter over medium-high heat. Add the ham and brown for 3 to 4 minutes per side. Add the juice mixture to the skillet, cover, and bring to a boil. Reduce the heat to low and simmer, covered, for 25 minutes. Add the pineapple slices and cherries; mix well. Cook, uncovered, for 8 to 10 more minutes, or until the sauce thickens and the fruit is heated through.

Apple-Raisin Glazed Ham

10 to 12 servings

This is no "pig tale"—for an easy and fancy-looking main dish, there's nothing better than a dressed-up ham!

One 5- to 6-pound fully
  cooked boneless
  cured ham
1 jar (18 ounces) apple jelly,
  divided
¼ cup firmly packed light
  brown sugar
1½ teaspoons dry mustard,
  divided
¾ cup apple juice
1 cup raisins
1 cinnamon stick
2 tablespoons cornstarch

Preheat the oven to 350°F. Place the ham in a 9" × 13" roasting pan that has been coated with nonstick cooking spray. In a small bowl, combine 2 tablespoons apple jelly, the brown sugar, and ½ teaspoon mustard; mix well. Spread evenly over the ham and bake for 50 to 60 minutes, or until heated through. In a small saucepan, cook the apple juice, raisins, and cinnamon stick over medium heat for 3 to 5 minutes, or until the raisins are plump. Add the remaining apple jelly and 1 teaspoon mustard and cook for 1 to 2 minutes, or until the jelly is melted; remove and discard the cinnamon stick. In a small bowl, combine the cornstarch with 3 tablespoons of the sauce from the saucepan; stir until smooth, then add to the saucepan and stir until the sauce is thickened. Remove the ham to a cutting board and slice. Serve with the sauce.

Hearty Ham Pie

6 to 8 servings

You've gotta make this, 'cause not only does it go together quickly, but you get to tell the kids it's okay to have pie for dinner!

2 cans (10¾ ounces each) condensed Cheddar cheese soup
½ cup milk
½ cup sour cream
½ teaspoon black pepper

4 cups cubed cooked ham
1 package (16 ounces) frozen broccoli cuts, thawed and drained
1 package (10 ounces) refrigerated pizza crust

Preheat the oven to 350°F. In a large bowl, combine the soup, milk, sour cream, and pepper; mix well. Stir in the ham and broccoli; mix well. Spoon into a 9" × 13" baking dish that has been coated with nonstick cooking spray. Unroll the pizza crust and cut crosswise into eleven 1-inch strips. Place 5 strips lengthwise over the top of the ham mixture, leaving a space between each strip. Place the remaining 6 strips crosswise over the top, forming a crisscross pattern. Bake for 30 to 35 minutes, or until the crust is golden and the casserole is heated through. Serve immediately.

Baked Ham in Cheese Crust

Once again I want to thank a viewer for sharing her recipe for Sunday dinner with me. It's nice to be let in on family secrets!

One 5-pound fully cooked
  canned ham
1 can (20 ounces) crushed
  pineapple, drained
1 cup (4 ounces) shredded
  Swiss cheese

1 cup plain dry bread crumbs
6 tablespoons (¾ stick)
  butter, melted
2 tablespoons dry mustard

Preheat the oven to 325°F. Place the ham in a roasting pan that has been coated with nonstick cooking spray. In a large bowl, combine the remaining ingredients; mix well. Using your hands, form a crust by patting the pineapple mixture over the ham, completely covering the top and sides. Bake for 1 to 1¼ hours, or until the ham is heated through and the crust is golden. Slice and serve.

Glazed Smoked Picnic Ham

6 to 8 servings

Don't pass this recipe by, 'cause you're gonna love that the glaze slowly caramelizes as it bakes, sealing in the ham's natural juices.

1½ cups ketchup
1 cup white vinegar
1 small onion, finely chopped
½ cup Worcestershire sauce
3 tablespoons prepared yellow mustard

3 tablespoons light brown sugar
¼ teaspoon black pepper
One 8- to 10-pound smoked picnic ham

Preheat the oven to 350°F. In a medium-sized bowl, combine all the ingredients except the ham; mix well. Place the ham in a roasting pan that has been lined with aluminum foil and coated with nonstick cooking spray. Pour the ketchup mixture over the ham. Bake for 2½ to 3 hours, or until the ham is glazed, basting every 30 minutes.

Country Ham Breakfast with Red-eye Gravy

5 servings

A great way to team biscuits, country ham, coffee, and grits.

1 package (10.8 ounces)
   refrigerated buttermilk
   biscuits (5 biscuits)
1 pound sliced country ham,
   rinsed, dried, and cut into
   serving-sized pieces

1 cup black coffee
1 teaspoon sugar
2½ cups warm cooked grits

Bake the biscuits according to the package directions. In a large skillet, cook the ham pieces a few at a time over medium heat for 3 to 4 minutes per side, or until browned on both sides. Transfer the cooked pieces to a serving plate and set aside. Add the coffee and sugar to the skillet and cook for 2 to 3 minutes, stirring to loosen the pan drippings. Continue cooking until the red-eye gravy is bubbling, stirring constantly. Split the biscuits and divide the ham equally among them. Serve with bowls of the grits topped with the red-eye gravy.

Glazed Leg of Lamb

10 to 12 servings

It would be a shame for you to skip this recipe 'cause you think a whole leg of lamb is too much for your family. Go ahead and make it for Sunday night's dinner. Then you'll have a bonus when you use the leftover cooked lamb for a few toss-together meals during the coming week.

1 garlic clove, minced
½ teaspoon dried thyme
2 teaspoons salt
½ teaspoon black pepper

One 7- to 9-pound leg of
  lamb, trimmed
1 jar (18 ounces) grape jelly
¼ cup apple cider vinegar

Preheat the oven to 325°F. In a small bowl, combine the garlic, thyme, salt, and pepper. Rub evenly over the leg of lamb and place in a roasting pan that has been lined with aluminum foil and coated with nonstick cooking spray. Bake for 2 hours. In a medium-sized bowl, whisk together the jelly and vinegar until thoroughly combined. Remove the leg of lamb from the oven and brush all over with the jelly mixture, turning to coat completely. Return the leg of lamb to the oven and bake for 30 more minutes for medium, or until desired doneness beyond that, basting the lamb every 15 minutes.

The Hen House

Main-Dish Poultry

The One and Only Fried Chicken

4 to 6 servings

There's nothing that says Southern cooking more than fried chicken—and this is the recipe you'll want to make over and over!

One 3- to 3½-pound chicken, cut into 8 pieces
3 teaspoons salt, divided
1½ cups all-purpose flour
¾ teaspoon black pepper
2 cups vegetable shortening

Place the chicken in a large bowl and add enough water to cover. Add 2 teaspoons salt and soak for 20 minutes. In a shallow dish, combine the flour, the remaining 1 teaspoon salt, and the pepper; mix well. Remove the chicken from the water and dip in the flour mixture, coating completely. In a large deep skillet, heat the shortening over medium heat until hot but not smoking. Place the coated chicken in the skillet in batches and fry for 8 to 10 minutes per side, or until golden and the juices run clear. Drain on a paper towel-lined platter. Serve immediately.

Note: To make the perfect gravy, drain off most of the oil from the skillet, leaving 1 to 2 tablespoons in the skillet along with any browned flour. Stir in an additional 3 tablespoons flour, ½ teaspoon salt, and ¼ teaspoon black pepper; cook over high heat until browned, stirring frequently. Whisk in 2 cups of milk and cook until smooth and thickened, whisking constantly. Serve with the fried chicken.

Chicken with Peanuts

Drive through the southern tier and you'll see field after field of peanut farms. That easily explains why they're featured in Southern cooking.

2 pounds boneless, skinless chicken thighs
1 teaspoon salt
¼ teaspoon black pepper
¼ cup (½ stick) butter
1 can (14½ ounces) diced tomatoes, drained, juice reserved

½ cup chunky peanut butter (see Note)
½ cup chicken broth
1 teaspoon sugar
2 medium-sized onions, chopped

Season the chicken with the salt and pepper. In a large skillet, melt the butter over medium heat. Add the chicken and brown for 8 to 10 minutes, turning to brown on all sides. Meanwhile, in a medium-sized bowl, combine the reserved tomato juice, the peanut butter, chicken broth, and sugar; mix well. Stir in the onions and tomatoes. Pour into the skillet and bring to a boil. Reduce the heat to low, cover, and simmer for 10 to 15 more minutes, or until no pink remains in the chicken.

Note: Don't have chunky peanut butter? Use creamy instead and add ¼ cup chopped peanuts, or just leave the peanuts out completely.

Creamy Chicken Bake

With all the poultry farms down South, chicken is practically a staple. So it's a given that I'd find loads of super chicken dishes like this one to share with you.

2 cups crushed butter-
 flavored crackers
¼ cup (½ stick) butter,
 melted
6 boneless, skinless chicken
 breast halves (1½ to 2
 pounds total)

¼ teaspoon salt
¼ teaspoon black pepper
1 can (10¾ ounces)
 condensed cream of
 chicken soup
1 cup sour cream
¼ cup water

Preheat the oven to 350°F. In a medium-sized bowl, combine the crushed crackers and butter; mix well. Spread half of the cracker mixture evenly over the bottom of a 9" × 13" baking dish that has been coated with nonstick cooking spray. Season the chicken on both sides with the salt and pepper and place in the baking dish over the cracker mixture. In a medium-sized bowl, combine the soup, sour cream, and water; mix well. Pour the soup mixture evenly over the chicken. Top with the remaining cracker mixture. Bake for 45 to 50 minutes, or until no pink remains in the chicken.

Note: Serve this over rice and sprinkle with some chopped fresh parsley to complete the dish.

Country Chicken and Rice

6 to 8 servings

Give this tasty Low Country dish a try. It's also known as "pilau" and "bogs," and it's a fill-you-up hearty dish that goes together so simply.

One 3- to 3½-pound chicken, cut into 8 pieces
6 cups water
2 cans (15 ounces each) tomato sauce
1 large onion, finely chopped

¼ teaspoon dried thyme
1 tablespoon salt
2 teaspoons black pepper
3 cups long- or whole-grain rice, rinsed

In a large pot, bring all the ingredients except the rice to a boil over medium-high heat. Cover and allow to boil for 35 minutes. Add the rice and cook for 25 to 30 minutes, or until the rice is tender and no pink remains in the chicken and the juices run clear.

Chicken Pot Pie Casserole

6 to 8 servings

Know what's better than a pot pie we can pick up at the market? One that we've made in our own kitchen—'cause there's just no beating our own homemade taste!

1½ pounds boneless, skinless chicken breasts, cut into 1-inch chunks
1 package (16 ounces) frozen mixed vegetables, thawed
1 can (14½ ounces) ready-to-use chicken broth

1 can (10¾ ounces) condensed cream of chicken and broccoli soup
2 cups biscuit baking mix
1½ cups milk
½ cup (1 stick) butter, melted

Preheat the oven to 350°F. In a large bowl, combine the chicken chunks, mixed vegetables, chicken broth, and soups; mix well. Spoon into a 9" × 13" baking dish that has been coated with nonstick cooking spray. In a medium-sized bowl, whisk the biscuit baking mix, milk, and butter until smooth and spoon over the top of the chicken mixture. Bake for 50 to 55 minutes, or until no pink remains in the chicken and the topping is golden.

Note: This can also be made in small round casserole dishes for individual pot pies.

Peachy Glazed Chicken

4 to 6 servings

This is for all you "Georgia peaches," wherever you are!

¼ cup all-purpose flour
¼ teaspoon ground ginger
½ teaspoon salt
¼ teaspoon black pepper
One 3- to 3½-pound chicken, cut into 8 pieces
¼ cup (½ stick) butter

1 can (29 ounces) sliced peaches in heavy syrup, undrained (see Note)
2 tablespoons soy sauce
2 tablespoons orange marmalade

In a large resealable plastic storage bag, combine the flour, ginger, salt, and pepper; mix well. Add the chicken pieces a few at a time and shake to coat completely; reserve the remaining flour mixture. In a large skillet, melt the butter over medium-high heat. Add the chicken and cook for 8 to 10 minutes, turning to brown on all sides; drain off any fat. Stir in the peaches and syrup, the soy sauce, marmalade, and the reserved flour mixture and bring to a boil. Reduce the heat to medium-low, cover, and simmer for 50 to 60 minutes, or until no pink remains in the chicken and the juices run clear. Serve with the sauce and peaches spooned over the chicken.

Note: Make sure to use peaches in heavy syrup for a nice thick sauce.

Shortcut Chicken 'n' Dumplings

4 to 6 servings

No need to spend hours over a hot stove to make this well-known dish. We're takin' a shortcut or two. Shh . . . no one will know the difference!

1½ pounds boneless, skinless chicken breasts, cut into 2-inch chunks
2 cans (14½ ounces each) reduced-sodium ready-to-use chicken broth
1 cup water

¼ cup (½ stick) butter
¼ teaspoon black pepper
1 package (7½ ounces) refrigerated biscuits (10 biscuits), each biscuit quartered

In a large pot, bring all the ingredients except the biscuits to a boil over high heat. Reduce the heat to low, cover, and simmer for 25 to 30 minutes, or until no pink remains in the chicken. Uncover and return to a boil over medium-high heat. Gently stir the biscuit quarters into the pot. Cook for 8 to 10 minutes, or until they are cooked through and the broth has thickened to form a gravy. Serve the chicken in bowls with the dumplings and gravy.

Mustard-Pecan Chicken Fillets

The gang'll go nuts over the way this is prepared! The crunchy coating is the key to the flavors of the whole dish!

4 boneless, skinless chicken breast halves (1 to 1½ pounds total), pounded to ¼-inch thickness

½ teaspoon salt
¼ cup molasses
¼ cup Dijon-style mustard
1½ cups chopped pecans

Preheat the oven to 350°F. Season the chicken breasts with the salt. In a shallow dish, combine the molasses and mustard; mix until well combined. Place the pecans in another shallow dish. Dip the chicken in the molasses mixture, then in the pecans, coating completely. Place the chicken in a 9" × 13" baking dish that has been coated with nonstick cooking spray. Bake for 35 to 40 minutes, or until no pink remains in the chicken.

Souped-up Chicken and Rice

6 to 8 servings

I've traveled quite a bit, and practically everyone has his or her own special chicken and rice dish. The secret to this one? It's "soup-er"!

1½ pounds boneless, skinless chicken breasts, cut into 1-inch chunks
2 cups water
1 can (10¾ ounces) condensed cream of chicken soup

1 can (4 ounces) mushroom stems and pieces, drained
1 cup long- or whole-grain rice
1 envelope (1 ounce) onion soup mix

Preheat the oven to 350°F. In a large bowl, combine all the ingredients; mix well. Spoon into a 9" × 13" baking dish that has been coated with nonstick cooking spray. Cover tightly with aluminum foil and bake for 1 to 1¼ hours, or until the rice is tender and no pink remains in the chicken.

Note: For a little color and a whole lot of flavor, sometimes I sprinkle some shredded sharp Cheddar cheese over the top before serving.

Apricot-Yam Chicken Bake

4 to 6 servings

Yams are as Deep South as you can get, and when they're roasted with chicken and glazed with the sweetness of apricots and their nectar, you're in for a treat!

2 cans (15 ounces each) yams, drained (see Note, page 239)
1 package (6 ounces) dried apricots
1 can (5.5 ounces) apricot nectar

One 3- to 3½-pound chicken, cut into 8 pieces
⅛ teaspoon cayenne pepper
½ teaspoon salt
¼ teaspoon black pepper
1 cup firmly packed light brown sugar

Preheat the oven to 375°F. In a 9" × 13" baking dish that has been coated with nonstick cooking spray, combine the yams, apricots, and nectar; mix well. Place the chicken over the yam mixture and sprinkle with the cayenne pepper, salt, and black pepper. Sprinkle the sugar over the top and bake for 55 to 60 minutes, or until no pink remains in the chicken and the juices run clear, basting twice during cooking.

Note: I've also made this with dried mixed fruit for a little additional color and flavor. Either way, it sure is good.

Pleasin' Beefy Chicken Bake

6 servings

What do we do when the gang can't agree on beef or chicken for dinner? We give 'em exactly what they want—an easy one-pot dish that'll please one and all!

1 jar (2¼ ounces) dried beef, rinsed and chopped
6 boneless, skinless chicken breast halves (1½ to 2 pounds total)
¼ teaspoon black pepper

1 can (10¾ ounces) condensed cream of chicken soup
1 cup sour cream
2 tablespoons real bacon bits

Preheat the oven to 350°F. Spread the chopped dried beef over the bottom of a 9" × 13" baking dish that has been coated with nonstick cooking spray. Season the chicken breasts with the pepper and place over the beef. In a medium-sized bowl, combine the soup and sour cream; mix well and pour over the chicken. Sprinkle with the bacon bits and cover tightly with aluminum foil. Bake for 50 minutes. Uncover and bake for 10 to 15 more minutes, or until no pink remains in the chicken. Stir the sauce and spoon over the chicken before serving.

Note: Make sure to cook a large batch of egg noodles or some rice to serve with this so you can enjoy every last bit of sauce.

Tangy Buttermilk Chicken

6 servings

Smooth, thick, and tangy, buttermilk makes this dish a taste sensation!

1 cup all-purpose flour
½ teaspoon garlic powder
1 teaspoon salt
¼ teaspoon black pepper
2 cups buttermilk, divided
¼ cup (½ stick) butter, melted

6 boneless, skinless chicken breast halves (1½ to 2 pounds total)
1 can (10¾ ounces) condensed cream of chicken soup

Preheat the oven to 425°F. In a shallow dish, combine the flour, garlic powder, salt, and pepper. Place ½ cup buttermilk in another shallow dish. Pour the melted butter over the bottom of a 9" × 13" baking dish. Dip the chicken in the buttermilk, then in the flour mixture, coating completely. Place in the baking dish and bake for 30 minutes. Turn the chicken and bake for 15 more minutes. In a medium-sized bowl, combine the soup and the remaining 1½ cups buttermilk. Pour evenly over the chicken. Bake for 15 to 20 minutes, or until heated through and no pink remains in the chicken.

Note: Sprinkle with some thinly sliced scallions just before serving to make this dish really come alive.

Creamy Chicken Casserole

4 to 6 servings

Let me tell you that Southerners really know how to make tasty casseroles. You've gotta give this one a try!

2 cups chunked cooked chicken
1 can (10¾ ounces) condensed chicken and rice soup
1 can (10¾ ounces) condensed cream of mushroom soup

1 can (5 ounces) evaporated milk
1 package (5 ounces) chow mein noodles

Preheat the oven to 350°F. In a large bowl, combine all the ingredients; mix well. Spoon into an 8-inch square baking dish that has been coated with nonstick cooking spray. Bake for 45 to 50 minutes, or until heated through.

Note: You can also add some drained sliced water chestnuts or frozen snow peas to add even more cross-cultural flavor to this casserole.

Cheesy Chicken Bundles

4 servings

Make way for these golden flaky pockets oozing with hot bubbly filling! They go great with a garden-fresh salad on the side.

2 cans (5 ounces each) chunk
    chicken, drained and
    flaked
1 package (3 ounces) cream
    cheese, softened

2 scallions, thinly sliced
⅛ teaspoon black pepper
1 package (8 ounces)
    refrigerated crescent rolls

Preheat the oven to 350°F. In a medium-sized bowl, combine
the chicken, cream cheese, scallions, and pepper; mix well.
Unroll the crescent rolls and separate the dough into 4 rectan-

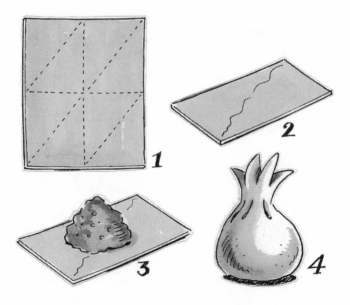

gles, pressing together 2 triangles for each rectangle. Place one quarter of the chicken mixture in the center of each rectangle. Pull the 4 corners of each together, forming bundles and pinching to seal (see illustration). Place on a baking sheet that has been coated with nonstick cooking spray and bake for 20 to 25 minutes, or until golden.

Note: I like to make these bundles in all sorts of different flavors. Sometimes I add ¼ teaspoon curry powder for Curried Chicken Bundles. Other additions you can try include ¼ cup chopped pecans, a drained 2-ounce jar of chopped pimientos, or ¼ cup chopped dried apricots.

Baked Cheesy Chicken

6 servings

This combination of dressing and cereal with chicken might sound a bit unusual, but let me tell you, the results are nothing less than luscious!

1 cup Russian dressing
2½ cups crispy rice cereal,
   coarsely crushed
1 cup grated Parmesan cheese

6 boneless, skinless chicken
   breast halves (1½ to 2
   pounds total)
2 tablespoons butter, melted

Preheat the oven to 350°F. Place the Russian dressing in a shallow dish. In another shallow dish, combine the crushed cereal and Parmesan cheese; mix well. Dip the chicken in the dressing, then in the cereal mixture, coating completely. Place on a baking sheet that has been coated with nonstick cooking spray. Drizzle the butter over the chicken and bake for 20 to 25 minutes, or until no pink remains in the chicken.

Note: If Russian dressing isn't your preferred flavor, you can use any type of creamy dressing like ranch or sweet-and-spicy French.

Orange-Glazed Cornish Hens

2 to 4 servings

These taste like a kiss of sunshine. Cut 'em in half or serve whole if you want your very own hen!

2 Cornish hens
1 teaspoon salt
¼ cup (½ stick) butter, melted
1 cup orange marmalade
2 tablespoons red wine vinegar

2 teaspoons Worcestershire sauce
½ teaspoon ground ginger
⅛ teaspoon cayenne pepper

Preheat the oven to 350°F. Rub the Cornish hens evenly with the salt and place breast side down in a 7" × 11" baking dish that has been lined with aluminum foil. Pour the melted butter over the hens. In a small bowl, combine the marmalade, vinegar, Worcestershire sauce, ginger, and cayenne pepper; mix well. Pour evenly over the Cornish hens and bake for 30 minutes. Turn the hens over and baste with the pan juices. Cook for 25 to 30 more minutes, or until the Cornish hens are no longer pink and the juices run clear. Serve whole or cut in half, and spoon the pan juices over the hens.

Note: To give these really intense sweet 'n' spicy flavor, use ¼ teaspoon cayenne pepper.

Mustard-Wine Cornish Hens

2 to 4 servings

No, I didn't mess up by putting the bread stuffing on top of the hens instead of inside! I found that the bread and mustard mixture prevents the hens from overbrowning, while keeping them juicy.

2 Cornish hens
1 teaspoon salt
¼ teaspoon black pepper
¼ cup prepared yellow
    mustard

3 slices white bread, torn into
    small pieces
2 scallions, finely chopped
2 tablespoons butter, melted
1 cup dry white wine

Preheat the oven to 400°F. Rub the Cornish hens evenly with the salt and pepper, then with the mustard. In a small bowl, combine the bread, scallions, and butter; mix well. Pat the bread mixture over the breasts of the Cornish hens and place in a 7" × 11" baking dish that has been coated with nonstick cooking spray. Pour the wine into the bottom of the baking dish and cover tightly with aluminum foil. Bake for 45 to 50 minutes, or until no pink remains in the Cornish hens. Remove the aluminum foil and bake for 10 to 15 more minutes, or until golden and the juices run clear. Serve whole or cut in half, and spoon the pan juices over the hens.

Note: Any type of soft bread can be used, including whole wheat or multigrain bread, which will give the stuffing additional flavor.

The Fishing Boat

Fish and Seafood

Fried Catfish

6 servings

Fish fries are as commonplace in the South as clambakes are in New England. They're often the focal point of church fund-raisers and other town social events.

1 egg	½ cup all-purpose flour
2 tablespoons prepared yellow mustard	1 teaspoon salt
1 tablespoon hot pepper sauce	1 cup vegetable oil
1 cup self-rising cornmeal	6 catfish fillets (about 2 pounds total)

In a shallow dish, combine the egg, mustard, and hot pepper sauce; mix well. In another shallow dish, combine the cornmeal, flour, and salt; mix well. In a large deep skillet, heat the oil over medium-high heat until hot but not smoking. Dip the catfish fillets in the egg mixture, then in the cornmeal mixture, coating completely. Cook the fillets a few at a time for 2 to 3 minutes per side, or until golden and the fish flakes easily with a fork. Drain on a paper towel–lined platter. Serve immediately.

Note: If you prefer baked catfish instead of fried, preheat the oven to 400°F. Coat the fillets as above, then place on a rimmed baking sheet that has been coated with nonstick cooking spray. Coat the tops of the fillets with nonstick cooking spray and bake for 12 to 15 minutes, or until the fish flakes easily with a fork. Serve immediately.

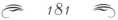

Cheesy Baked Flounder

6 servings

Floundering for just the right fish for dinner? Look no further—
you've found it!

¼ cup vegetable oil
1 cup cornflake crumbs
½ cup grated Parmesan
  cheese
½ teaspoon salt, divided

½ teaspoon black pepper,
  divided
6 flounder fillets (about 2
  pounds total)
Nonstick cooking spray

Preheat the oven to 400°F. Place the oil in a shallow dish. In
another shallow dish, combine the cornflake crumbs, cheese,
¼ teaspoon salt, and ¼ teaspoon pepper; mix well. Season the
flounder fillets with the remaining ¼ teaspoon salt and ¼ teaspoon pepper. Dip the seasoned fillets in the oil, then in the
crumb mixture, coating completely. Place on large rimmed baking sheets that have been coated with nonstick cooking spray.
Lightly coat the top of the fillets with nonstick cooking spray
and bake for 12 to 15 minutes, or until the coating is golden
and the fish flakes easily with a fork. Serve immediately.

Note: You can buy cornflake crumbs or make your own by
crushing cornflakes very fine.

Trout Fish Fry

8 servings

'Round some parts, it's customary for trout to be raised in hatcheries, then released into mountain streams where fishing's allowed for certain sizes only! Here's a fine way to serve up that trout "catch of the day"!

¼ teaspoon dry mustard
¼ teaspoon dried basil
¼ teaspoon cayenne pepper
¼ teaspoon salt

8 trout fillets (about
 2 pounds total)
3 egg yolks
1½ cups cornflake crumbs
Vegetable oil for frying

In a shallow dish, combine the mustard, basil, cayenne pepper, and salt; mix well. Remove half of the seasoning mixture and use to season the trout fillets on both sides. Beat the egg yolks into the remaining seasoning mixture. Place the cornflake crumbs in another shallow dish. In a large deep skillet, heat 1 inch of oil over high heat until hot but not smoking. Dip the trout fillets in the seasoned egg mixture, then in the cornflake crumbs, coating completely. Cook the fillets a few at a time for 3 to 4 minutes per side, or until the coating is golden and the fish flakes easily with a fork. Serve immediately.

Note: If you prefer baked instead of fried fish, preheat the oven to 400°F. Coat the fillets as above and place on a rimmed baking sheet that has been coated with nonstick cooking spray. Drizzle 3 tablespoons melted butter over the tops of the fillets and bake for 10 to 12 minutes, or until the fish flakes easily with a fork. Serve immediately.

Blackened Catfish

Today most of the catfish available in our supermarkets is farm-raised, which means it's a more delicate, flavorful fish than the muddy-tasting catfish of years ago. And when we blacken it quickly at a really high temperature, we're in for a big treat!

4 teaspoons paprika
2 teaspoons dried thyme
1 teaspoon onion powder
1 teaspoon garlic powder
1 teaspoon sugar

¼ teaspoon cayenne pepper
1 teaspoon salt
1 teaspoon black pepper
6 catfish fillets (about
    2 pounds total)

In a shallow dish, combine all the ingredients except the catfish; mix well. Dip the catfish fillets in the seasoning mixture, coating both sides completely. Heat a large skillet over high heat until very hot but not smoking. Place the catfish in the hot skillet a few at a time and cook for 2 to 3 minutes per side, or until the coating is blackened and the catfish flakes easily with a fork. Serve immediately.

Note: Coat the fillets generously with the seasoning mixture, but don't worry—you'll taste spiciness, but this blackened catfish won't be *too* spicy. Traditionally, this is made in a cast-iron skillet, but any type of skillet should work.

Carolina Crab-Stuffed Flounder

6 servings

Did you know that native South Carolinians are entitled to haul in two buckets of crabs a year as their birthright?! No wonder they've created such yummy crab recipes—like this one that we can all enjoy, no matter how far we live from the ocean!

6 tablespoons (¾ stick) butter, divided
1 celery stalk, finely chopped
1 small onion, finely chopped
¼ cup chopped fresh parsley
1 can (4¼ ounces) crabmeat, drained and flaked
½ cup plain dry bread crumbs
1 tablespoon lemon juice
⅛ teaspoon cayenne pepper
6 flounder fillets (about 2 pounds total)
¼ teaspoon paprika

Preheat the oven to 400°F. In a large skillet, melt 4 tablespoons butter over medium-high heat. Add the celery, onion, and parsley and sauté for 5 to 6 minutes, or until the celery and onion are tender. Remove from the heat and stir in the crabmeat, bread crumbs, lemon juice, and cayenne pepper. Spoon the crabmeat mixture evenly over the fillets. Starting from a small end, roll up each fillet jelly-roll style. Place the rolls seam side down in a 9" × 13" baking dish that has been coated with non-stick cooking spray. Melt the remaining 2 tablespoons butter and drizzle over the fillets; sprinkle the tops with the paprika. Bake for 20 to 25 minutes, or until the fish flakes easily with a fork. Serve immediately.

Citrus Trout Fillets

8 servings

Wow—this sure is fresh-tasting! Well, between the sliced lemon and the fresh parsley, it's a sure winner.

¼ cup (½ stick) butter, melted
½ teaspoon salt
⅛ teaspoon black pepper

8 trout fillets (about 2 pounds total) (see Note)
4 large lemons, thinly sliced
¼ cup chopped fresh parsley

Preheat the oven to 400°F. In a shallow dish, combine the butter, salt, and pepper; mix well. Dip the trout fillets in the butter mixture and place on large rimmed baking sheets. Completely cover the tops of the trout fillets with the lemon slices and sprinkle with the parsley. Bake for 12 to 15 minutes, or until the fish flakes easily with a fork. Serve immediately.

Note: Try to find a fish market that has fresh trout. Keep the fish on ice till you're ready to coat it. The sooner you make this after buying the fish, the better!

Purr-fect Catfish Fingers

6 to 8 servings

Today catfish is farm-raised, but in the past it was common to catch a few of them by hand while bass fishing. Of course, if you're gonna do that, you've gotta be careful not to get bitten by their sharp teeth! So, once you've got the catfish (whether you buy 'em or catch 'em), fry 'em up this way and . . . well, let's just say you'll be the cat's meow!

2 eggs
¼ cup sour cream
1½ teaspoons cayenne
  pepper, divided
1½ teaspoons dried oregano,
  divided

1 teaspoon salt, divided
2 cups self-rising cornmeal
1½ cups vegetable oil
2 pounds catfish fillets, cut
  into 1-inch strips

In a shallow dish, whisk together the eggs, sour cream, ½ teaspoon cayenne pepper, ½ teaspoon oregano, and ¼ teaspoon salt; beat well. In another shallow dish, combine the cornmeal and the remaining 1 teaspoon cayenne pepper, 1 teaspoon oregano, and ¾ teaspoon salt; mix well. In a large skillet, heat the oil over medium-high heat until hot but not smoking. Dip the catfish fingers in the egg mixture, then in the cornmeal mixture, coating completely. Cook the catfish fingers in batches for 2 to 3 minutes per side, or until the coating is golden and the fish flakes easily with a fork. Drain on a paper towel–lined platter. Serve immediately.

Note: These are so good that I like to eat them plain, but feel free to serve 'em with your favorite dipping sauce.

No-Fuss Salmon Casserole

Hit the pantry instead of the high seas for the main ingredient in this "quickie" that's so rich and thick it tastes like a hearty soup.

2 cans (15½ ounces each) red salmon, drained and flaked (skin and bones discarded)

2 cans (10¾ ounces each) condensed cream of celery soup

1 can (14½ ounces) sliced carrots, drained

4 cups cooked elbow macaroni

1 small onion, finely chopped

1 cup (4 ounces) shredded sharp Cheddar cheese

1 cup milk

¼ teaspoon black pepper

½ cup plain dry bread crumbs

2 tablespoons butter, melted

Preheat the oven to 375°F. In a large bowl, combine the salmon, soup, carrots, macaroni, onion, cheese, milk, and pepper; mix well. Spoon into a 9" × 13" baking dish that has been coated with nonstick cooking spray. In a small bowl, combine the bread crumbs and butter; mix well and sprinkle evenly over the casserole. Bake for 45 to 50 minutes, or until heated through and the topping is golden.

Note: I like to use a good-quality red salmon to make this a really flavorful casserole, but any variety of canned salmon will work.

Tuna Tarts

Eat these right out of the oven for a quick dinner, or serve them at room temperature with a side of fruit salad for a ladies' luncheon.

2 cans (6 ounces each) tuna, drained and flaked
¾ cup chopped peanuts
1 package (3 ounces) cream cheese, softened
¼ cup mayonnaise
1 teaspoon prepared yellow mustard
¼ teaspoon garlic powder
1 package (7½ ounces) refrigerated biscuits (10 biscuits)
¼ cup all-purpose flour

Preheat the oven to 400°F. In a medium-sized bowl, combine the tuna, peanuts, cream cheese, mayonnaise, mustard, and garlic powder; mix well. Flour a work surface and a rolling pin, then roll out each biscuit to a 5-inch circle. Line 10 muffin cups with the flattened biscuits, forming crusts. Fill the crusts equally with the tuna mixture and bake for 12 to 15 minutes, or until the crusts are golden. Serve warm.

Note: This can also be made with canned chunk chicken and pecans or other types of nuts.

Salmon Patties

1 dozen

Pure and simple—served with a cool crisp salad, these make a perfect summer supper.

2 cans (15½ ounces each) red salmon, drained and flaked (skin and bones discarded)	½ teaspoon baking powder
	1 teaspoon onion powder
	½ teaspoon salt
2 eggs	½ teaspoon black pepper
1 cup all-purpose flour	¼ cup vegetable oil

In a large bowl, combine all the ingredients except the oil; mix well and form into 12 equal patties. In a large skillet, heat the oil over medium-high heat until hot but not smoking. Cook the patties in batches for 1 to 2 minutes per side, or until golden. Drain on a paper towel–lined platter. Serve immediately.

Note: Here's an easy dill sauce to serve with these patties: In a small bowl, combine 1 cup sour cream, ½ cup mayonnaise, 1 tablespoon sweet pickle relish, 2 teaspoons lemon juice, and 1 teaspoon dried dillweed. Mix well and chill for at least 1 hour before serving.

Mouthwatering Crab Cakes

1 dozen

Soft on the inside, crunchy on the outside . . . these are exactly the way we want 'em!

3 cans (4¼ ounces each) crabmeat, drained and flaked
2 cups Italian-flavored bread crumbs, divided
¼ cup (½ stick) butter, softened
3 eggs
1 celery stalk, finely chopped
3 tablespoons mayonnaise
1½ teaspoons Worcestershire sauce
1 teaspoon salt
½ teaspoon black pepper
¼ cup vegetable oil

In a medium-sized bowl, combine the crabmeat, 1¼ cups bread crumbs, the butter, 2 eggs, the celery, mayonnaise, Worcestershire sauce, salt, and pepper; mix well. Shape into 12 crab cakes, using about ¼ cup of the mixture for each. In a shallow dish, beat the remaining egg with a fork. Place the remaining ¾ cup bread crumbs in another shallow dish. In a large skillet, heat the oil over medium heat until hot but not smoking. Dip the crab cakes in the egg, then in the bread crumbs, coating completely. Cook the crab cakes in batches for 3 to 4 minutes per side, or until golden. Drain on a paper towel–lined platter. Serve immediately.

Note: Although many restaurants in the South serve these with a spicy sauce, I think they're best served plain so you can really taste the crab.

Perfect Fried Shrimp

4 to 6 servings

Most every Southern coastal town has loads of fresh shrimp available—and with frying being a favorite regional preparation, the two go hand in hand!

¾ cup all-purpose flour
1 tablespoon baking powder
1 teaspoon salt
1 teaspoon cayenne pepper
2 eggs

¼ cup milk
½ cup vegetable oil
1½ pounds large shrimp,
    peeled and deveined, tails
    left on

In a shallow dish, combine the flour, baking powder, salt, and cayenne pepper; mix well. In another shallow dish, beat the eggs and milk with a fork until well combined. In a large skillet, heat the oil over medium-high heat until hot but not smoking. Dip the shrimp in the flour mixture, then in the egg mixture, and then again in the flour mixture, coating completely. Cook the shrimp for about 1 minute per side, or until the coating is golden and the shrimp are cooked through. Drain on a paper towel–lined platter. Serve immediately.

Note: Cocktail sauce, tartar sauce, or any of your favorite dipping sauces can be served with these shrimp. You might even want to try some of the sauces from the barbecue chapter.

Spicy Boiled Shrimp

4 to 6 servings

Just mention a shrimp boil and watch everyone come running. So my advice is: Don't be skimpy when planning the amount of shrimp!

8 cups water
1 small onion, chopped
¼ cup red wine vinegar
¼ cup seafood seasoning
2 tablespoons butter

1 teaspoon hot pepper sauce
1½ pounds large shrimp, peeled and deveined, tails left on

In a large pot, bring all the ingredients except the shrimp to a boil over high heat. Remove from the heat, add the shrimp, cover, and let stand for 10 to 15 minutes to cook the shrimp and to allow the flavors to marry.

Note: There's really only one way to enjoy these—served with the broth in a bowl over rice. I like them with hearty bread for dunking, too.

Plantation Shrimp Cocktail

4 to 6 servings

Look at the docks off Georgia or the Carolinas and you'll see lots of shrimping boats. What better way to serve up all that luscious shrimp than in a shrimp cocktail where the shrimp has cooked in cocktail sauce with veggies. Mmm!

8 cups water
1 small onion, chopped
1 celery stalk, chopped

1½ pounds large shrimp, peeled and deveined, tails left on
1 jar (12 ounces) cocktail sauce

In a large pot, bring the water, onion, and celery to a boil over medium-high heat. Add the shrimp and cook for 2 to 3 minutes, or until the shrimp turn pink; drain. Return the shrimp and vegetables to the pot, add the cocktail sauce, and cook over medium heat for 2 to 4 minutes to blend the flavors. Transfer to a bowl and chill for at least 1 hour before serving.

Note: Use iceberg lettuce leaves to create a bowl for this that's both colorful and edible. It's a perfect appetizer or even a light dinner.

Spicy Crunchy Oysters

3 to 4 servings

The cornmeal-and-spice coating gives these oysters a true down-home taste.

1 egg
¼ cup milk
½ teaspoon salt
¼ teaspoon black pepper
½ cup all-purpose flour
½ cup cornmeal

¼ teaspoon cayenne pepper
½ cup vegetable oil
2 containers (8 ounces each)
  shucked fresh oysters,
  rinsed and drained
  (see Note, page 45)

In a shallow dish, combine the egg, milk, salt, and black pepper; mix well. In another shallow dish, combine the flour, cornmeal, and cayenne pepper; mix well. In a large skillet, heat the oil over medium-high heat until hot but not smoking. Dip the oysters one at a time in the egg mixture, then in the cornmeal mixture, coating completely. Cook the coated oysters a few at a time for 3 to 4 minutes per side, or until golden. Drain on a paper towel–lined platter. Serve immediately.

Note: It's traditional to squeeze half a lemon over the oysters and serve them with cocktail sauce.

Scalloped Oysters

4 to 6 servings

No mystery about this fancy-sounding name. "Scalloped" means a food that's combined with a sauce and topped with cracker or bread crumbs—and that's just how we bake up this one!

1 sleeve (4 ounces) saltine crackers, divided	2 cups milk
2 tablespoons butter, melted	4 eggs
1 container (8 ounces) shucked fresh oysters, rinsed and drained (see Note, page 45)	1 teaspoon salt
	1 teaspoon black pepper

Preheat the oven to 375°F. In a small bowl, crush 8 crackers and add the butter; mix well and set aside. In a 2-quart casserole

dish, layer half of the remaining crackers with half of the oysters; repeat the layers. In a medium-sized bowl, beat the milk, eggs, salt, and pepper with a fork until well combined. Pour over the oysters and crackers. Sprinkle the reserved cracker mixture over the casserole and bake for 30 to 35 minutes, or until heated through and the topping is golden.

Note: Always be sure to keep oysters well chilled and use them within a day or two.

Fried Oysters

3 to 4 servings

Our Southeastern coast produces lots of oysters for us, and I can't think of a better way to enjoy them than lightly fried and crispy on the outside, hot and creamy on the inside.

3 egg whites
1 teaspoon salt, divided
1 teaspoon black pepper, divided
1 cup cracker meal (see Note)

½ cup vegetable oil
2 containers (8 ounces each) shucked fresh oysters, rinsed and drained (see Note, page 45)

In a medium-sized bowl, whisk together the egg whites, ½ teaspoon salt, and ½ teaspoon pepper until well beaten. In a shallow dish, combine the cracker meal and the remaining ½ teaspoon salt and ½ teaspoon pepper. In a large skillet, heat the oil over medium-high heat until hot but not smoking. Dip the oysters one at a time in the egg mixture, then in the cracker meal mixture, coating completely. Cook the coated oysters a few at a time for 3 to 4 minutes per side, or until the coating is golden. Drain on a paper towel–lined platter. Serve immediately.

Note: Cracker meal is finely ground cracker crumbs; it can be found near the bread crumbs in the supermarket.

Gardens and Fields
Vegetable and Fruit Side Dishes

continued

Asparagus Casserole

What a great accent for a special meal!

6 ounces butter-flavored crackers (half of a 12-ounce package)

2 cans (15 ounces each) asparagus spears, drained, ½ cup liquid reserved

1½ cups (6 ounces) shredded sharp Cheddar cheese, divided

1 can (10¾ ounces) condensed cream of mushroom soup

Preheat the oven to 350°F. In a 2-quart casserole dish that has been coated with nonstick cooking spray, layer one quarter of the crackers, one third of the asparagus, and one third of the cheese. Repeat the layers two more times and top with the remaining crackers. In a medium-sized bowl, combine the soup and the reserved ½ cup asparagus liquid; mix well. Pour evenly over the casserole and bake for 30 to 35 minutes, or until heated through and the top is golden.

Home-Baked Beans

Once you've tried these, plain old out-of-the-can baked beans will be a thing of the past. The long, slow oven cooking helps the flavors cook to perfection!

6 slices bacon, diced
2 cans (16 ounces each)
  baked beans (any variety)
1 medium-sized onion, finely
  chopped
1½ cups ketchup

¼ cup molasses
3 tablespoons prepared
  yellow mustard
3 tablespoons light brown
  sugar
2 garlic cloves, minced

Preheat the oven to 375°F. In a large skillet, cook the bacon over medium heat for 6 to 8 minutes, or until crisp, stirring frequently. Remove from the heat and add the remaining ingredients; mix well. Spoon into a 9" × 13" baking dish that has been coated with nonstick cooking spray. Bake for 60 to 70 minutes, or until the juices are thickened and bubbly.

Note: For an even easier dish, sometimes I use one 3-ounce container of real bacon bits instead of cooking bacon. Then all you need to do is mix and bake.

Black-eyed Peas

Yes, you can make black-eyed peas starting with dried peas that you have to pick over, soak, and boil till tender. But why do all that when you can start with frozen and have these yummies on the table in less than an hour?

2 tablespoons butter
1 small onion, chopped
1 can (10½ ounces) condensed chicken broth
½ cup water

1 package (16 ounces) frozen black-eyed peas, thawed
1 large tomato, cut into large chunks
½ teaspoon salt

In a large saucepan, melt the butter over medium-high heat and sauté the onion for 3 to 4 minutes, or until tender. Add the remaining ingredients and bring to a boil. Reduce the heat to medium-low and cook for 45 to 50 minutes, until the tomato has cooked down to form a sauce, stirring occasionally.

Creamed Cabbage

Garden fresh and "un-be-leaf-ably" good!

1 large head cabbage,
    coarsely chopped
1 medium-sized onion,
    chopped
1 cup water
1 teaspoon salt

¼ teaspoon black pepper
1 can (10¾ ounces)
    condensed cream of
    mushroom soup
1 jar (2 ounces) chopped
    pimientos, drained

In a large pot, bring the cabbage, onion, water, salt, and pepper to a boil over medium-high heat. Cover and allow to boil for 10 minutes. Drain off the water and add the soup and pimientos; mix well. Reduce the heat to low and simmer for 15 to 20 minutes, or until the cabbage is tender.

Fried Cabbage

Just turn up the heat and start the fryin'. Then watch them follow their noses right to the kitchen table!

¼ pound bacon

¼ cup (½ stick) butter

1 medium-sized head
   cabbage, coarsely chopped

1 teaspoon salt

¼ teaspoon black pepper

In a large pot, cook the bacon over medium-high heat until crisp. Remove the bacon from the pot; let cool, then crumble and set aside. Add the remaining ingredients to the pot. Reduce the heat to low, cover, and cook for 30 to 35 minutes, or until the cabbage is tender, stirring frequently. Sprinkle with the crumbled bacon, toss, and serve.

Butter-Glazed Carrots

6 to 8 servings

Everyone will ask you where you found carrots so tender and sweet. If they only knew the answer!

½ cup sugar
¼ cup white vinegar
¼ cup (½ stick) butter
¼ cup water

½ teaspoon cornstarch
4 cans (14½ ounces each)
    sliced carrots, drained

In a medium-sized saucepan, bring the sugar, vinegar, and butter to a boil over medium heat. In a small bowl, combine the water and cornstarch, stirring until the cornstarch is dissolved. Add the cornstarch mixture to the vinegar mixture, stirring until thickened. Add the carrots, cover, and cook for 5 to 7 minutes, or until heated through.

Note: For the best flavor, after cooking the carrots, allow them to cool, then chill overnight. This allows the carrots to marinate and really absorb the other flavors. When ready to serve, just reheat.

Cheesy Cauliflower

A melty Cheddar cheese sauce baked over tender cauliflower makes the perfect side dish to go along with fresh ham or roast chicken.

¼ cup (½ stick) butter
2 packages (16 ounces each) frozen cauliflower florets, thawed
1 tablespoon all-purpose flour

¼ teaspoon cayenne pepper
¾ teaspoon salt
2 cups (8 ounces) shredded sharp Cheddar cheese
¾ cup milk

In a large saucepan, melt the butter over medium heat. Add the cauliflower, flour, cayenne pepper, and salt, stirring until well mixed. Reduce the heat to medium-low, add the cheese and milk, and simmer for 8 to 10 minutes, or until the cheese is melted and the sauce has thickened, stirring frequently.

Steamin' Collards

Whether you pick up some collard greens at the produce counter or at a roadside farm stand, you're gonna be in for a really fresh-tasting side dish!

1 bunch collard greens (about 2 pounds), stems removed and coarsely chopped

One 2-ounce piece salt pork
1 tablespoon sugar
1½ teaspoons salt

In a large pot, combine all the ingredients over medium-high heat. Add just enough water to cover. Bring to a boil, then cover and cook for 1½ to 2 hours, or until the collards are tender, stirring occasionally.

Note: Here's a little tip I learned that'll help reduce the odor when cooking collards: In a second large pot, boil 8 cups water with ½ cup white vinegar. Keep the 2 pots boiling at the same time and they'll offset each other's odor. (I've heard that doing that keeps flies away, too!)

Country Corn

This recipe is as simple as it sounds—even with chopping the corn first. Know why we have to do that? Well, let's just say that it makes the corn taste sweeter and creamier than you could ever have imagined. Those Southerners are pretty clever when it comes to their veggies.

2 packages (16 ounces each)   ½ teaspoon salt
   frozen corn kernels, thawed   ¼ teaspoon black pepper
6 tablespoons (¾ stick) butter

In a blender or a food processor that has been fitted with its metal cutting blade, process each package of corn separately until coarsely chopped, scraping down the bowl as needed (see Note). Transfer to a large saucepan and add the remaining ingredients. Cook over medium heat for 6 to 8 minutes, or until heated through, stirring constantly.

Note: If using a blender, process in stages for just a few seconds at a time, making sure to scrape down the container several times while processing so that all the corn is coarsely chopped. But don't overdo it, or you'll end up with mush!

Home-Style Corn Pudding

The English brought their version of corn pudding to the South, and this is my simple takeoff on the international and regional favorite.

2 cans (15 ounces each)
  cream-style corn
½ cup heavy cream
2 eggs, beaten
1 tablespoon all-purpose
  flour

1 tablespoon sugar
¼ teaspoon cayenne pepper
2 cups coarsely crushed
  butter-flavored crackers
3 tablespoons butter, melted

Preheat the oven to 350°F. In a medium-sized bowl, combine the corn, heavy cream, eggs, flour, sugar, and cayenne pepper; mix well. Pour into a 2-quart casserole dish that has been coated with nonstick cooking spray. In a medium-sized bowl, combine the crushed crackers and butter; sprinkle evenly over the corn mixture. Bake for 40 to 45 minutes, or until heated through and the topping is golden. Allow to stand for 5 minutes before serving.

Baked Eggplant

I remember how I used to stand over the stove and fry sliced eggplant a few pieces at a time. Oh, what a mess it was to clean up! Well, I'm not doing that anymore. Baked is the only way for me!

¾ cup seasoned bread crumbs
½ cup mayonnaise

1 medium-sized eggplant, peeled and cut into ¼-inch slices

Preheat the oven to 350°F. Place the bread crumbs in a shallow dish. Spread the mayonnaise evenly on both sides of the eggplant slices, then coat completely with the bread crumbs. Place on a large rimmed baking sheet that has been coated with non-stick cooking spray and bake for 30 to 35 minutes, or until the eggplant is tender and the coating is golden.

Note: If you soak the sliced eggplant in cold salted water for about ½ hour, then pat it dry before breading it, that should take away some of its sharp taste.

Cheesy Eggplant-Squash Bake

6 to 8 servings

It's easy to get everybody to eat their veggies when we serve 'em up in such an appealing combination. Southern cooks have been making this dish for years, and now we're lucky to be in on their secret.

½ cup (1 stick) butter
1 medium-sized eggplant, peeled and cut into ½-inch chunks
4 medium-sized yellow squash, cut into ½-inch chunks
2 medium-sized onions, chopped

1½ cups milk
2 eggs
2 cups (8 ounces) shredded sharp Cheddar cheese, divided
½ cup instant rice
½ teaspoon salt
½ teaspoon black pepper

Preheat the oven to 350°F. In a large skillet, melt the butter over medium-high heat. Add the eggplant, squash, and onions and sauté for 6 to 8 minutes, or until the vegetables are slightly tender. Meanwhile, in a large bowl, combine the milk, eggs, 1½ cups cheese, the rice, salt, and pepper; mix well. Add the vegetable mixture to the egg mixture; mix well. Pour into a 3-quart casserole dish that has been coated with nonstick cooking spray. Sprinkle the remaining ½ cup cheese over the top and bake for 50 to 55 minutes, or until the rice is tender.

Southern Green Bean Casserole

9 to 12 servings

What makes this Southern-style? It's the addition of two extras—cream cheese and buttery cracker crumbs!

1 can (10¾ ounces)
  condensed cream of
  mushroom soup
1 package (8 ounces) cream
  cheese, softened
½ teaspoon salt
4 packages (9 ounces each)
  frozen French-cut green
  beans, thawed and drained

1 cup crushed butter-flavored
  crackers
¼ cup (½ stick) butter,
  melted

Preheat the oven to 350°F. In a large bowl, combine the soup, cream cheese, and salt; mix well. Stir in the beans and spoon into a 9" × 13" baking dish that has been coated with nonstick cooking spray. In a medium-sized bowl, combine the crushed crackers and butter; mix well. Sprinkle the cracker mixture evenly over the beans and bake for 25 to 30 minutes, or until heated through and the topping is golden.

Steamin' Taters 'n' Beans

6 to 8 servings

Sometimes simple is best . . . like here we've got fresh green beans and red potatoes boiled up with a little salt pork. Mmm, mmm!

One 2-ounce piece salt pork
2 pounds fresh green beans,
   trimmed and cut in half
½ teaspoon black pepper

12 small red potatoes (about
   2 pounds), cut in half
2 teaspoons salt

Place the salt pork, green beans, and pepper in a large pot and add enough water to cover. Place the potatoes on top and sprinkle with the salt. Cover loosely and bring to a boil over high heat. Reduce the heat to low and simmer for 30 to 35 minutes, or until the potatoes and beans are tender. Serve in bowls with the broth.

Note: In the South, they call the broth "pot liquor" and serve it with plenty of corn bread for dunking.

Fried Okra

Sometimes it's not easy to find small, tender okra—you know, the really mild-flavored ones—so I just use larger ones and cut them up. They're easy enough to slice and fry the same as we'd do the little ones.

¼ cup all-purpose flour
½ cup yellow cornmeal
⅛ teaspoon cayenne pepper
1½ teaspoons salt, divided

1 pound fresh okra, trimmed
  and cut into ½-inch slices
2 cups vegetable oil

In a large resealable plastic storage bag, combine the flour, cornmeal, cayenne pepper, and 1 teaspoon salt; mix well. Rinse and drain the okra slices, then add to the bag, seal, and shake to coat thoroughly with the flour mixture. In a large pot, heat the oil over high heat until hot but not smoking. Add half of the coated okra and cook for 5 to 6 minutes, or until golden. With a slotted spoon, remove the okra to a paper towel–lined platter to drain. Repeat with the remaining coated okra. Sprinkle the fried okra with the remaining ½ teaspoon salt and serve.

Boiled Okra

Enjoy this versatile veggie simply boiled this way all by itself, or add some to your soups and stews to thicken and flavor them up.

8 cups water
1 pound fresh okra, rinsed
    and trimmed

2 teaspoons salt
¼ cup (½ stick) butter

In a large saucepan, combine the water, okra, and salt; bring to a boil over high heat. Allow to boil for 3 to 4 minutes, or until the okra is tender. Drain, then return the okra to the saucepan. Add the butter and cook over low heat until the butter melts and coats the okra, stirring frequently.

Note: These are a favorite when cooked just right, but be careful not to overcook them—that makes 'em get slimy and turn to mush.

Cracker-Onion Pie

6 to 8 servings

It's a cinch to work with onions—just slice off the stem end, peel back the paper-thin layers, and start slicing. After you taste this great main meal go-along, there are sure to be no more tears!

1 cup crushed saltine crackers
⅔ cup butter, divided
2 large onions, thinly sliced
  (see Note)
4 eggs

1 cup milk
1 teaspoon salt
½ teaspoon black pepper
½ cup (2 ounces) shredded
  sharp Cheddar cheese

Preheat the oven to 350°F. In a medium-sized bowl, combine the crushed crackers and ⅓ cup melted butter. Press over the bottom and up the sides of a 9-inch pie plate that has been coated with nonstick cooking spray, forming a crust. In a large skillet, over medium-high heat, sauté the onions in the remaining ⅓ cup butter for 12 to 15 minutes, or until the onions are tender. Carefully pour the onion mixture into the crust. In a medium-sized bowl, use a fork to thoroughly beat the eggs, milk, salt, and pepper; pour over the onions. Sprinkle the cheese over the top and bake for 40 to 45 minutes, or until the top is golden and the center is set. Let stand for 5 minutes, then cut into wedges and serve.

Note: I like to use Vidalia onions in this pie for an unbeatable sweet onion flavor.

English Pea Casserole

Here's a spin-off of a Southern recipe that shows the influence of the English settlers.

1 can (10¾ ounces)
   condensed cream of
   mushroom soup
1 can (15 ounces) peas,
   drained
1 can (8 ounces) sliced water
   chestnuts, drained
1 jar (2 ounces) chopped
   pimientos, drained

1 small onion, finely
   chopped
1 cup (4 ounces) shredded
   sharp Cheddar cheese
1 cup crushed butter-flavored
   crackers
6 tablespoons (¾ stick)
   butter, melted

Preheat the oven to 350°F. In a medium-sized bowl, combine the soup, peas, water chestnuts, pimientos, and onion. Spoon into an 8-inch square baking dish that has been coated with nonstick cooking spray. Sprinkle with the cheese. In a medium-sized bowl, combine the crushed crackers and butter; mix well and sprinkle evenly over the casserole. Bake for 25 to 30 minutes, or until heated through and the topping is golden.

Simple Rutabagas

Today the big push is for each of us to eat at least five servings of fruit and veggies a day. Well, that's nothing new in the South, 'cause no Sunday meal was ever complete without at least three different veggies. Good old rutabagas will be a great change-of-pace dish for many of us!

2 large rutabagas (about 4
   pounds total), peeled and
   cut into 1-inch chunks
One 4-ounce piece salt pork,
   cut into ½-inch chunks

3 cups water
1 teaspoon sugar
1 teaspoon salt
½ teaspoon black pepper

In a large pot, bring all the ingredients to a boil over medium-high heat. Reduce the heat to medium, cover, and cook for 45 to 50 minutes, or until tender. Drain and serve.

Spinach Casserole Surprise

They'll be green with envy when they find out that you made this specialty all by yourself!

1 package (3 ounces) cream
   cheese, softened
¼ cup (½ stick) butter,
   softened
½ teaspoon salt
¼ teaspoon black pepper

2 packages (10 ounces each)
   frozen chopped spinach,
   thawed and well drained
¼ cup grated Parmesan
   cheese
¼ cup chopped pecans

Preheat the oven to 350°F. In a large bowl, combine the cream cheese, butter, salt, and pepper; mix well. Add the spinach; mix well. Spoon into a 1½-quart casserole dish that has been coated with nonstick cooking spray. Sprinkle with the cheese, then with the pecans. Bake for 30 to 35 minutes, or until heated through and the top is golden.

Creamed Spinach

I was lucky enough to have this family recipe sent to me from one of my Tennessee viewers about four years ago. I'm sure glad I held on to it!

2 packages (10 ounces each) frozen chopped spinach, thawed and well drained
½ of a small onion, finely chopped
½ cup (1 stick) butter, melted, divided

¼ cup heavy cream
⅓ cup grated Parmesan cheese
½ cup crushed butter-flavored crackers

Preheat the oven to 350°F. In a medium-sized bowl, combine the spinach, onion, 5 tablespoons butter, the heavy cream, and Parmesan cheese. Spoon into an 8-inch square baking dish that has been coated with nonstick cooking spray. In a small bowl, combine the remaining 3 tablespoons butter and the crushed crackers and sprinkle evenly over the spinach mixture. Bake for 15 to 20 minutes, or until heated through and the topping is golden.

Saucy Squash Bake

4 servings

Serve the taste of a holiday any night of the week. (It looks pretty holiday-fancy, too!)

2 acorn squash, cut in half
   and seeded (see Note)
1 cup applesauce
¼ cup firmly packed light
   brown sugar

2 tablespoons butter,
   softened
1½ teaspoons ground
   cinnamon

Preheat the oven to 400°F. Place the squash cut side up in a 9" × 13" baking dish that has been coated with nonstick cooking spray. Spoon the applesauce equally into the cavities of the squash. In a small bowl, combine the remaining ingredients; mix until crumbly. Sprinkle over the top of the squash and bake for 60 to 65 minutes, or until the squash is tender.

Note: Cut a small piece off the bottom of the squash halves so they'll sit flat in the baking dish.

Hearty Squash Casserole

4 to 6 servings

This is a side dish often found at Southern "supper gatherings." It's chock-full of melty cheese and crunchy pecans, and it's bound to make a squash lover out of everyone!

2 eggs
1 tablespoon sugar
1½ cups (6 ounces) shredded sharp Cheddar cheese, divided
½ cup mayonnaise
½ teaspoon salt

¼ teaspoon black pepper
1 package (16 ounces) sliced yellow squash, thawed and drained
¾ cup chopped pecans
¼ cup plain dry bread crumbs

Preheat the oven to 350°F. In a large bowl, with a fork, beat the eggs and sugar until frothy. Add 1 cup cheese, the mayonnaise, salt, and pepper; mix well. Stir in the squash and pecans until thoroughly combined. Pour into a 1½-quart casserole dish that has been coated with nonstick cooking spray. In a small bowl, combine the bread crumbs and the remaining ½ cup cheese and sprinkle over the top of the squash mixture. Bake for 25 to 30 minutes, or until heated through and the cheese is golden.

Squash Puff Cakes

about 1 dozen

Fritters are no stranger to the South, and they certainly aren't limited to squash. Yummy fried corn and eggplant puffs are also often found on tables throughout the region.

2 packages (16 ounces each) frozen yellow squash, thawed, drained, and chopped
1 egg, beaten

⅓ cup biscuit baking mix
¾ teaspoon salt
¼ teaspoon black pepper
About 3 tablespoons vegetable oil

In a large bowl, combine all the ingredients except the oil; mix well. Heat 1 tablespoon oil in a large skillet over medium heat. Pour ¼ cup of the batter into the skillet to form each cake. Cook for 3 to 4 minutes per side, or until golden. Remove to a paper towel–lined platter and cover to keep warm. Repeat until all the batter is used, adding more oil as needed.

Note: If you prefer to use fresh squash instead of frozen, coarsely chop 3 to 4 medium-sized yellow squash and sauté in a little oil until tender. Then continue as above.

Fried Green Tomatoes

6 to 8 servings

I'm not talking about a movie here . . . although I did really enjoy the movie by this name! I'm talkin' about crispy, crunchy fried slices of green tomatoes—a real staple of the South.

1 egg
¼ cup water
1½ teaspoons salt
½ teaspoon black pepper
5 medium-sized green tomatoes, cored and cut into ¼-inch slices (see Note)

1 cup all-purpose flour
1 cup self-rising white cornmeal mix
1½ cups vegetable oil

In a large bowl, combine the egg, water, salt, and pepper; mix well. Add the tomato slices and toss to coat well. In a shallow dish, combine the flour and cornmeal mix; mix well. Dip a tomato slice into the flour mixture, coating completely, and place on a baking sheet. Repeat until all of the slices are coated. In a large skillet, heat the oil over high heat until hot but not smoking. Fry the coated tomatoes a few at a time for 2 to 3 minutes per side, or until golden. Drain on a paper towel–lined platter. Serve warm.

Note: Green tomatoes?? Sure, they're available in the early summer in most markets, but with their popularity growing all around the country, you can often find them during the rest of the year in specialty and health food markets. My suggestion is

to ask your regular supermarket produce manager for them.
Oh—allowing the first slices to sit on the baking sheet while the
rest are coated will help the breading stay on. (So fry the first
ones you coated first.) These are great as is or served with a
creamy horseradish sauce.

Boiled Turnip Greens

Very, very Southern-simple, so why not have these veggies "turn up" on your family's plates tonight? They're a super change of pace!

2 packages (16 ounces each)
   frozen chopped turnip
   greens, thawed (see Note)
One 4-ounce piece salt pork

¼ cup water
2 tablespoons butter
1¼ teaspoons salt
¼ teaspoon black pepper

In a large pot, bring all the ingredients to a boil over high heat. Reduce the heat to medium, cover, and cook for 25 to 30 minutes, or until the turnip greens are tender, stirring occasionally.

Note: Sure, you can use 2 to 2½ pounds fresh turnip greens instead. Remove the stems and wash the greens. You can leave them whole or chop them; boil them until wilted, then drain. Return them to the pot and proceed as above.

Mixed-Up Veggie Casserole

6 to 8 servings

Grab the trivet and set the casserole dish on the table. It's time for a mixed-up dinner!

2 cans (15 ounces each) mixed vegetables, drained
1 can (8 ounces) sliced water chestnuts, drained
1 jar (2 ounces) chopped pimientos, drained
1 medium-sized onion, chopped
2 stalks celery, chopped
1 can (10¾ ounces) condensed cream of chicken soup
¾ cup mayonnaise
2 cups (8 ounces) shredded sharp Cheddar cheese, divided

Preheat the oven to 350°F. In a large bowl, combine the mixed vegetables, water chestnuts, pimientos, onion, and celery; mix well. Stir in the soup, mayonnaise, and 1 cup Cheddar cheese; mix until well combined. Spoon into a 3-quart baking dish that has been coated with nonstick baking spray. Sprinkle evenly with the remaining 1 cup cheese, cover, and bake for 30 minutes. Uncover and bake for 10 to 15 more minutes, or until heated through and the cheese is golden.

Cran-Apple Casserole

6 to 8 servings

This is ideal for a buffet dinner. Just fix it in advance, cover it and pop it in the fridge, then bake it right before the gang arrives! Can you keep a secret? This is so fruity and gooey, I've even served it over scoops of vanilla ice cream. Boy, has *that* gotten rave reviews!

4 medium-sized apples, peeled, cored, and chopped
2 cups fresh cranberries (see Note)
1½ cups granulated sugar
⅓ cup all-purpose flour
1½ cups quick-cooking or old-fashioned rolled oats

½ cup firmly packed light brown sugar
½ cup coarsely chopped pecans
½ cup (1 stick) butter, melted

Preheat the oven to 350°F. In a large bowl, combine the apples, cranberries, granulated sugar, and flour. Spoon into an 8-inch square baking dish that has been coated with nonstick cooking spray. In a medium-sized bowl, combine the remaining ingredients; mix well. Spread the oat mixture evenly over the fruit mixture. Bake for 60 to 65 minutes, or until golden and bubbly.

Note: If fresh cranberries aren't available, you can always use 2 cups of frozen cranberries that have been thawed.

Warm Apple Rings

4 to 6 servings

If you like baked apples, you're gonna love these—fried and all buttery-sweet!

¼ cup (½ stick) butter
4 large apples, cored and cut
   into ¼-inch rings

⅓ cup firmly packed light
   brown sugar
1 teaspoon ground cinnamon

In a large skillet, melt the butter over medium-low heat. Add the apple rings and cook for 12 to 15 minutes, or until the apples are tender, stirring to coat the apples with the butter. In a small bowl, combine the brown sugar and cinnamon; mix well and sprinkle over the apples. Cook for 2 to 3 minutes, or until the sugar dissolves into the butter and creates a thickened syrup. Serve the apples immediately, topped with the syrup.

Note: The perfect side dish for a country ham dinner, or even for breakfast . . . yup, breakfast.

Curried Fruit

Hand me my sunglasses 'cause this fruit is bursting with bright color . . . *and* taste. It's the best go-along for poultry of any kind!

1 cup firmly packed light
   brown sugar
½ cup (1 stick) butter
1 tablespoon curry powder
2 cans (15 ounces each) pear
   halves, drained
1 can (29 ounces) peach
   halves, drained

1 can (20 ounces) pineapple
   slices, drained
1 can (15 ounces) apricot
   halves, drained
1 jar (6 ounces) maraschino
   cherries, drained

Preheat the oven to 325°F. In a medium-sized saucepan, combine the brown sugar, butter, and curry powder over medium heat until the butter is melted and the sugar is dissolved, stirring constantly; remove from the heat. In a 9" × 13" baking dish, combine the remaining ingredients; mix well. Pour the brown sugar mixture over the fruit and bake for 55 to 60 minutes, or until hot and bubbly. Serve immediately.

Note: Either cold or slightly warm, leftovers make a great ice cream topping!

Cheesy Baked Pineapple

9 to 12 servings

The dishes of the South are loaded with cheese because of the abundance of dairy cows raised there. Well, that bounty of cheese sure does wonders for *this* recipe. Don't pass it by!

2 cans (20 ounces each) pineapple chunks, drained
2 cups (8 ounces) shredded sharp Cheddar cheese
½ cup sugar

3 tablespoons all-purpose flour
2 cups coarsely crushed butter-flavored crackers
½ cup (1 stick) butter, melted

Preheat the oven to 350°F. Place the pineapple in a 9" × 13" baking dish that has been coated with nonstick cooking spray. In a medium-sized bowl, combine the cheese, sugar, and flour. Sprinkle the cheese mixture evenly over the pineapple. In another medium-sized bowl, combine the crushed crackers and butter; mix well. Sprinkle the cracker mixture over the casserole and bake for 25 to 30 minutes, or until heated through and the topping is golden.

Hearty Go-Alongs

Potatoes, Rice, and Pasta

Cheddar Potato Casserole

Sometimes we need that special side dish and simply don't have enough time to get it together. Well, that won't happen with this one.

3½ cups water
½ cup (1 stick) butter
1 teaspoon salt
½ teaspoon black pepper
3½ cups instant potato flakes

1 small onion, finely
   chopped
1½ cups (6 ounces) shredded
   sharp Cheddar cheese
1 cup (½ pint) heavy cream

Preheat the oven to 350°F. In a large saucepan, bring the water, butter, salt, and pepper to a boil over high heat. Remove the saucepan from the heat and stir in the potato flakes and onion; mix well. Spoon the potato mixture into an 8-inch square baking dish that has been coated with nonstick cooking spray. Sprinkle with the cheese and pour the cream over the top. Bake for 35 to 40 minutes, or until heated through and the edges are golden.

Note: For all of you who are skeptical about using instant potato flakes, go ahead and give 'em a try. You won't be disappointed.

Shredded Sweet Potatoes

6 to 8 servings

When I first tried these, I was shocked. Why? 'Cause they didn't look like the traditional sweet potatoes I was used to. But were they ever good . . . so good that now I make them this way on a regular basis!

4 medium-sized sweet
   potatoes (about 2 pounds),
   peeled and grated
1 tablespoon salt
1 cup sugar

½ cup light corn syrup
¼ cup water
¼ cup (½ stick) butter
1 cup pineapple juice

Preheat the oven to 375°F. Place the potatoes in a large bowl and sprinkle with the salt. Add enough ice water to just cover the potatoes and let stand for 10 minutes. Meanwhile, in a medium-sized saucepan, combine the sugar, corn syrup, and water; bring to a boil over medium-high heat, stirring constantly. Remove from the heat and stir in the butter and pineapple juice until the butter is melted. Drain the potatoes well and place in a 9" × 13" baking dish that has been coated with nonstick cooking spray. Pour the sugar mixture over the potatoes and bake for 55 to 60 minutes, or until the potatoes are tender, stirring halfway through the baking.

Note: If you prefer your potatoes a little less sweet, cut back on the sugar. The amount of sweetness is up to you.

Buttermilk-Topped Spuds

For a change from the ordinary, pass on the sour cream and dollop this buttermilk topper onto your baked potatoes!!

4 large baking potatoes	1 small onion, grated
½ cup mayonnaise	1 teaspoon garlic powder
½ cup buttermilk	

Preheat the oven to 400°F. Scrub the potatoes and pierce the skins several times with a fork; bake for 55 to 60 minutes, or until tender. In a small bowl, combine the remaining ingredients until well mixed. Cut the baked potatoes open and spoon the buttermilk mixture over the tops. Serve immediately.

Buttery Potato Balls

4 to 6 servings

These spuds will really shake things up—they'll add excitement to any meal. (And they're fun to make, too!)

½ cup (1 stick) butter, melted
2 cans (15 ounces each)
  whole small potatoes,
  drained

½ cup all-purpose flour
½ teaspoon onion powder
1 teaspoon salt
¼ teaspoon black pepper

Preheat the oven to 425°F. Place the butter in a shallow dish, add the potatoes, and roll to coat the potatoes completely with the butter. In a large resealable plastic storage bag, combine the remaining ingredients. Add the buttered potatoes to the bag and shake until thoroughly coated; reserve the butter in the dish. Remove the potatoes and shake off any excess flour. Roll the coated potatoes in the remaining butter and place on a large rimmed baking sheet that has been coated with nonstick cooking spray. Bake for 40 to 45 minutes, or until golden, turning halfway through the baking.

Note: If some of the potatoes are large, cut them into 1-inch chunks so that the pieces will all be about the same size.

Sweet Potato Casserole

Southerners sure have taken a liking to their sweet potatoes—and thank goodness they'll never stop creating new ways to serve them up!

1 cup chopped pecans
1 cup firmly packed light
 brown sugar
⅓ cup all-purpose flour
½ cup (1 stick) butter,
 softened, divided
2 cans (29 ounces each) sweet
 potatoes, drained and
 mashed (see Note)

¾ cup granulated sugar
2 eggs
½ cup milk
1 teaspoon vanilla extract
½ teaspoon salt

Preheat the oven to 350°F. In a medium-sized bowl, combine the pecans, brown sugar, flour, and ¼ cup butter; mix until crumbly, then set aside. In a large bowl, combine the remaining ingredients, including the remaining ¼ cup butter; mix well. Spoon into a 3-quart casserole dish that has been coated with nonstick cooking spray. Sprinkle the pecan mixture evenly over the potato mixture and bake for 45 to 50 minutes, or until heated through and bubbly.

Note: Canned sweet potatoes and yams are practically interchangeable, and in some parts of the country you can get only one or the other. Either one can be used in this recipe.

True Fried Grits

8 to 10 servings

Yup, this is the real thing—a down-home Southern classic with a today-easy twist!

5 cups water	2 tablespoons butter
1 teaspoon salt	2 tablespoons vegetable oil
1½ cups white or yellow grits	

In a medium-sized saucepan, bring the water and salt to a boil over medium heat. Stirring constantly, add the grits and cook for 8 to 10 minutes, or until the water is absorbed and the mixture is very thick. Spoon into a 9" × 5" loaf pan that has been lined with plastic wrap and coated with nonstick cooking spray. Cover and chill for at least 2 hours, or until ready to serve. When ready to serve, invert onto a cutting board and remove the plastic wrap; cut into ½-inch slices. In a large skillet, heat the butter and oil over medium heat until hot but not smoking. Fry the slices a few at a time for 2 to 3 minutes per side, or until golden. Serve immediately.

Note: Use only as many slices as you need and keep the remaining loaf in the refrigerator, well wrapped, until needed again. To make traditionally shaped fried grits, rinse several heavy glasses with water. Pack the warm grits firmly into the glasses and chill. Remove the entire log from the glass (or glasses) and slice off as much as you want, returning the rest to the fridge in the glass(es). Fry your round grits cakes as above. And if you're wondering what the difference is between the yellow and white grits, it's not only the color: The yellow ones have a stronger corn flavor.

Golden Grits Casserole

6 to 8 servings

There's more than one way to serve the Southern classic. Try this baked version for a delicious golden treat!

3½ cups water
1 cup white or yellow grits
1 cup (4 ounces) shredded
    sharp Cheddar cheese
6 tablespoons (¾ stick)
    butter, softened
⅔ cup milk

3 eggs, beaten
2 tablespoons Worcestershire
    sauce
⅛ teaspoon cayenne pepper
1 teaspoon salt
¼ teaspoon black pepper

Preheat the oven to 350°F. In a large saucepan, bring the water to a boil over high heat. Stirring constantly, add the grits and cook for 5 to 8 minutes, or until the water is absorbed and the mixture is very thick. Remove from the heat and add the cheese and butter; stir until melted and well combined. Stir in the remaining ingredients until well blended, then spoon into an 8-inch square baking dish that has been coated with nonstick cooking spray. Bake for 30 to 35 minutes, or until light golden.

Hush Puppies

about 2½ dozen

In the Old South, they used to make these yummy cornmeal balls so they'd have something to throw to the hounds to keep them from howling when Yankee soldiers approached. And if you've always wondered how they got their name, now you know!

2 cups self-rising cornmeal	¾ cup milk
1 medium-sized onion, finely chopped	1 egg
	Peanut oil for frying

In a medium-sized bowl, combine all the ingredients except the oil; mix well. In a large pot, heat 1 inch of oil over high heat until hot but not smoking. In batches, drop the cornmeal mixture by rounded teaspoonfuls into the oil to form the hush puppies. Cook for 2 to 3 minutes, turning to brown on all sides. Remove from the oil with a slotted spoon and drain on a paper towel–lined platter. Serve immediately.

Sage Corn Bread Dressing

6 to 8 servings

Use those day-old leftover corn muffins to make a go-along that's perfect for matching up with roast turkey. And if you drizzle the pan drippings over this, you'd better be ready for some really hearty eating!

6 cups coarsely crumbled
  corn muffins (see Note)
4 slices white bread, torn into
  small pieces
1 medium-sized onion,
  chopped

⅓ cup butter, melted
1 tablespoon rubbed sage
½ teaspoon black pepper
2 eggs, beaten
2 cans (14½ ounces each)
  ready-to-use chicken broth

Preheat the oven to 425°F. In a large bowl, combine the crumbled muffins, the bread, onion, butter, sage, and pepper. Add the eggs and broth, stirring until well combined. Pour into an 8-inch square baking dish that has been coated with nonstick cooking spray. Bake for 50 to 55 minutes, or until the dressing is golden and the edges are set.

Note: Six corn muffins (16 ounces total) will yield 6 cups crumbled; if you prefer, just crumble corn bread.

Welcome-Home Eggplant Casserole

4 to 6 servings

This one's fancy enough for the holidays. It sure has the comfort tastes we all crave when we want that "welcome home" feeling!

6 cups water
1 medium-sized eggplant, peeled and cut into 1-inch chunks
1 small onion, chopped
1 teaspoon salt
¼ teaspoon black pepper
1 can (10¾ ounces) condensed cream of mushroom soup

½ cup milk
1 egg
1 cup herb stuffing mix
2 cups (8 ounces) shredded sharp Cheddar cheese, divided

Preheat the oven to 350°F. In a large pot, combine the water, eggplant, onion, salt, and pepper; bring to a boil over high heat. Allow to boil for 10 to 12 minutes, or until the eggplant is tender. Drain and transfer the eggplant and onion to a large bowl. Add the soup, milk, egg, stuffing mix, and 1 cup cheese; mix well. Spoon into a 1½-quart casserole dish that has been coated with nonstick cooking spray. Sprinkle the remaining 1 cup cheese evenly over the eggplant mixture. Bake for 35 to 40 minutes, or until heated through and the edges are golden.

Mushroom Rice Bake

4 to 6 servings

Tradition in a Southern kitchen is to wash raw rice before cooking it. They say it makes the rice fluffier and more moist. Why not give it a try?

1½ cups long- or whole-
    grain rice
1 small onion, chopped
1 can (10½ ounces)
    condensed beef broth
1 can (10¾ ounces)
    condensed cream of
    mushroom soup

¼ cup (½ stick) butter,
    melted
½ teaspoon black pepper
¼ teaspoon paprika

Preheat the oven to 375°F. In a medium-sized bowl, combine all the ingredients except the paprika; mix well. Spoon into a 2-quart casserole dish that has been coated with nonstick cooking spray. Sprinkle the paprika evenly over the top. Cover and bake for 50 to 55 minutes, or until the liquid is absorbed and the rice is tender.

Note: For even more mushroom flavor, add a drained 4-ounce can of mushroom stems and pieces to the rice mixture.

Hoppin' John

4 to 6 servings

This is a New Year's Day favorite that's traditionally served with collard greens. The Hoppin' John is for good luck and the collards represent money that you hope to receive in the new year.

4 slices bacon, diced
1 medium-sized onion,
   chopped
1 teaspoon salt

½ teaspoon black pepper
1 can (15½ ounces) black-
   eyed peas
3 cups hot cooked rice

In a medium-sized saucepan, combine the bacon, onion, salt, and pepper over medium heat. Cook for 10 to 12 minutes, or until the bacon is crisp and the onion is golden, stirring frequently. Reduce the heat to low. Add the black-eyed peas and rice and stir for 2 to 3 minutes, or until heated through.

Note: I like to sprinkle this with a few drops of hot pepper sauce for added spiciness.

Snappy Broccoli Bake

6 to 8 servings

Oh, boy! This is a robust veggie bake that'll surely win you plenty of applause.

2 packages (10 ounces each) frozen chopped broccoli, thawed and well drained
2 cups cooked rice
1 container (16 ounces) processed cheese spread
1 can (10¾ ounces) condensed cream of mushroom soup

1 can (8 ounces) sliced water chestnuts, drained
½ teaspoon salt
¼ teaspoon black pepper
1 can (2.8 ounces) French-fried onions

Preheat the oven to 350°F. In a large bowl, combine all the ingredients except the French-fried onions; mix well until thoroughly combined. Pour into a 3-quart casserole dish that has been coated with nonstick cooking spray. Sprinkle the onions evenly over the top and bake for 30 to 35 minutes, or until golden and bubbly.

Yankee Doodle Macaroni Casserole

When Yankee Doodle went to town, maybe he was looking for a hot bubbly casserole brimming with cheese and macaroni, just like this one!

1 package (8 ounces) elbow macaroni

2 cups (8 ounces) shredded sharp Cheddar cheese

1 medium-sized onion, finely chopped

1 jar (2 ounces) chopped pimientos, drained

4 slices white bread, cut into small pieces

½ cup milk

¼ cup (½ stick) butter, melted

¼ cup chopped fresh parsley

3 eggs, beaten

½ teaspoon salt

⅛ teaspoon black pepper

Preheat the oven to 300°F. Cook the macaroni according to the package directions; drain, rinse, and drain again. In a large bowl, combine the remaining ingredients; mix well. Add the macaroni and mix until well combined. Spoon the mixture into an 8-inch square baking dish that has been coated with non-stick cooking spray. Bake for 50 to 55 minutes, or until the center is set.

Southern-Style Spaghetti Salad

6 to 8 servings

Here's a pasta salad that makes great use of an all-time favorite—spaghetti. And if you can, try not to gobble up all those yummy olives before you add them to the dish!

1 pound spaghetti, broken
  in half
2 cups (8 ounces) shredded
  Colby-Jack cheese
1 cup mayonnaise

1 jar (5 ounces) sliced
  Spanish olives, drained
2 tablespoons sweet pickle
  relish
½ teaspoon black pepper

Cook the spaghetti according to the package directions; drain. Meanwhile, in a large bowl, combine the remaining ingredients; mix well. Add the hot spaghetti and toss until well mixed. Serve warm.

Note: Leftovers also make a great chilled salad.

Crunchy Macaroni and Cheese

9 to 12 servings

For kids and adults who are big macaroni and cheese lovers, this baked dish is pure heaven. With the addition of crackers on top, it becomes a *crunchy,* creamy delight!

1 package (16 ounces) elbow macaroni
¾ cup (1½ sticks) butter, melted, divided
4 cups (16 ounces) shredded sharp Cheddar cheese
4 eggs, beaten
3 cups milk
½ teaspoon salt
½ teaspoon black pepper
24 saltine crackers

Preheat the oven to 350°F. Cook the macaroni according to the package directions; drain, rinse, and drain again. In a large bowl, combine the macaroni, ½ cup butter, the cheese, eggs, milk, salt, and pepper. Spoon the macaroni mixture into a 9" × 13" baking dish that has been coated with nonstick cooking spray. Place the crackers in a single layer over the top of the casserole and drizzle with the remaining ¼ cup melted butter. Bake for 35 to 40 minutes, or until heated through and the top is golden.

Note: This also makes a great main dish that can serve 4 to 6 people. You may want to use unsalted crackers if you're cutting down on your salt intake.

The Cake Shop

Cakes and Frostings

continued

Old-fashioned Southern Chocolate Cake

12 to 16 servings

One forkful of this mellow, light chocolate cake, and you'll be transplanted to a breezy porch on a Southern plantation!

2 cups all-purpose flour
¼ cup unsweetened cocoa
1 teaspoon baking soda
⅛ teaspoon salt
1 cup sugar
½ cup vegetable shortening
¼ cup (½ stick) butter,
    softened

4 eggs
1 cup buttermilk
2 teaspoons vanilla extract
Old-fashioned Southern
    Chocolate Frosting
    (page 254)

Preheat the oven to 350°F. In a medium-sized bowl, combine the flour, cocoa, baking soda, and salt; mix well and set aside. In a large bowl, with an electric beater on medium speed, beat the sugar, shortening, and butter until fluffy. Beat in the eggs until well mixed. Gradually beat in the flour mixture. Add the buttermilk and vanilla and beat until well mixed. Divide the batter between two 9-inch round cake pans that have been coated with nonstick cooking spray. Bake for 25 to 30 minutes, or until a wooden toothpick inserted in the center of each comes out clean. Let cool for 10 minutes, then invert onto wire racks to cool completely. Place 1 cake layer upside down on a serving platter and frost the top with the frosting. Place the second layer over the first and frost the top and sides. Serve, or cover loosely until ready to serve.

Old-fashioned Southern Chocolate Frosting

about 1½ cups

This glossy frosting is perfect for topping cakes that you want to fancy up with decorating gel.

¼ cup (½ stick) butter
1 can (5 ounces) evaporated milk
¼ cup granulated sugar

2 squares (1 ounce each) unsweetened chocolate
1¼ cups confectioners' sugar
1 teaspoon vanilla extract

In a small saucepan, combine the butter, evaporated milk, granulated sugar, and chocolate squares. Cook over medium-low heat until the chocolate has melted and the mixture has come to a low boil, stirring frequently. Reduce the heat to low and cook for 4 to 5 minutes, stirring constantly. Remove from the heat and add the confectioners' sugar and vanilla; mix well. Chill for 30 minutes to thicken before using.

Note: This isn't like traditional frosting; it's more of a cross between a glaze and a thick icing.

Cream Cheese Pound Cake

12 to 16 servings

This is a little richer than traditional pound cake, but it still has that same buttery taste. Since the cream cheese is already in it, you can serve it as is, or maybe top it with fresh-cut fruit or a scoop of butter pecan ice cream.

1½ cups (3 sticks) butter, slightly softened

1 package (8 ounces) cream cheese, softened

3 cups sugar

2 teaspoons vanilla extract

6 eggs

3 cups all-purpose flour

Preheat the oven to 275°F. In a large bowl, with an electric beater on medium speed, beat the butter and cream cheese until creamy. Beat in the sugar and vanilla until well mixed. Beat in the eggs one at a time. Gradually add the flour, beating until well combined. Pour the batter into a 10-inch Bundt or tube pan that has been coated with nonstick cooking spray. Bake for 1½ to 1¾ hours, or until a wooden toothpick inserted in the center comes out clean. Let cool for 10 minutes, then invert onto a wire rack to cool completely. Serve, or cover until ready to serve.

Strawberry Shortcake

9 servings

No meal in the South is complete without dessert, and it doesn't matter if it's a cookie, a bar, or a piled-high layer cake. But when I serve this classic made-from-scratch shortcake, all of a sudden it's everybody's first choice!

3 cups biscuit baking mix	3 tablespoons confectioners'
¼ cup granulated sugar	sugar
1 cup milk	1 quart fresh strawberries,
1 cup (½ pint) heavy cream	hulled and sliced

Preheat the oven to 350°F. In a medium-sized bowl, combine the baking mix, granulated sugar, and milk; mix well. Spread the batter in an 8-inch square baking dish that has been coated with nonstick cooking spray. Bake for 30 to 35 minutes, or until golden and a wooden toothpick inserted in the center comes out clean; let cool completely. In a large bowl, with an electric beater on medium speed, beat the heavy cream and confectioners' sugar until stiff peaks form. Cut the cake into 9 squares, then cut each square horizontally in half. Place the bottom squares on individual serving plates or a large serving platter and distribute the sliced strawberries and then the whipped cream mixture evenly over the tops, reserving some of each for garnish. Place the remaining cake squares on top. Top with the reserved whipped cream and strawberries. Serve, or cover loosely and chill until ready to serve.

Note: The best way to serve this strawberry shortcake is to prepare the shortcake, whipped cream, and strawberries. Then cut and assemble only as many servings as you need. Cover the remaining shortcake and chill the remaining whipped cream and strawberries until needed.

Watermelon Cake

12 to 16 servings

If you've driven through the farmlands of the South, you've most likely seen plenty of fields of cotton, tobacco, and plump, juicy watermelons. That's why it's no surprise that we came across this watermelon cake. The best part? It has no seeds!

1 package (18.25 ounces) white cake mix
1 package (4-serving size) watermelon-flavored gelatin (see Note)
1 tablespoon all-purpose flour
¾ cup vegetable oil

1½ cups cubed and seeded watermelon, well drained, divided
4 eggs
½ cup (1 stick) butter, softened
1 box (16 ounces) confectioners' sugar

Preheat the oven to 325°F. In a large bowl, with an electric beater on low speed, beat the cake mix, gelatin mix, flour, oil, and 1 cup watermelon until well mixed. Beat in the eggs one at a time until well blended. Divide the batter between two 9-inch round cake pans that have been coated with nonstick cooking spray. Bake for 40 to 45 minutes, or until a wooden toothpick inserted in the center of each comes out clean. Let cool for 10 minutes, then invert onto wire racks to cool completely. In a medium-sized bowl, with an electric beater on medium speed, beat the butter and sugar until well combined. Gradually beat in the remaining ½ cup watermelon until smooth. Place 1 cake layer upside down on a serving plate and frost the top with the watermelon frosting. Place the second layer over the first and frost the top and sides. Serve, or cover loosely until ready to serve.

Note: If you can't find watermelon-flavored gelatin, you can replace it with strawberry or mixed fruit. With the fresh watermelon in here, either of those flavors should work fine.

Peach Coffee Cake

12 to 15 servings

Wanna show them some real Southern hospitality? The next time friends come over for dessert, serve some peach coffee cake with a tall glass of Simply Refreshing Iced Tea (page 325) or Perky Cinnamon Water (page 324).

1¾ cups sugar, divided
1 cup plus 2 tablespoons (2¼ sticks) butter, softened, divided
3 eggs
3¼ cups all-purpose flour, divided

2 teaspoons baking powder
1 teaspoon vanilla extract
1 container (21 ounces) peach pie filling
¼ cup chopped pecans
¼ teaspoon ground nutmeg

Preheat the oven to 350°F. In a large bowl, with an electric beater on medium speed, beat 1½ cups sugar and 1 cup butter until creamy. Beat in the eggs one at a time, mixing well after each addition. Add 3 cups flour, the baking powder, and vanilla; beat well. Spread half of the batter in a 9" × 13" baking pan that has been coated with nonstick cooking spray. Spoon the peach pie filling evenly over the cake batter, leaving a ½-inch border around the edges. Drop the remaining batter by tablespoonfuls over the peach pie filling. Using a wet knife, carefully spread the batter, covering the peach pie filling completely. In a small bowl, combine the remaining ¼ cup sugar, ¼ cup flour, and 2 tablespoons butter, the pecans, and nutmeg until well mixed and crumbly. Sprinkle evenly over the top of the cake. Bake for 55 to 60 minutes, or until a wooden toothpick inserted in the center comes out clean.

Allow to cool slightly, then cut and serve, or cover until ready to serve.

Note: Of course, you can serve this at room temperature, or maybe heat it for a few seconds in the microwave or a few minutes in the oven just before serving.

Coconut Cake

12 to 16 servings

If you walked into any Southern bakery, or stopped by the local school bake sale, I'll bet you'd find an impressive coconut cake winking at you. But since most of us can't do that, we can bake it right at home.

1 package (18.25 ounces) white cake mix
1 cup water
½ cup coconut milk, divided
¼ cup vegetable oil
2 eggs

1 container (12 ounces) frozen whipped topping, thawed
1 package (6 ounces) frozen grated coconut, thawed

Preheat the oven to 350°F. In a large bowl, with an electric beater on medium speed, beat the cake mix, water, ¼ cup coconut milk, the oil, and eggs for 2 minutes, or until smooth. Divide the batter between two 9-inch round cake pans that have been coated with nonstick cooking spray. Bake for 25 to 30 minutes, or until a wooden toothpick inserted in the center of each comes out clean. Let cool for 10 minutes, then invert onto wire racks to cool completely. Using a fork, poke small holes in the bottom of each cake layer. Pour the remaining ¼ cup coconut milk evenly over the layers. Place 1 cake layer upside down on a serving plate and frost the top with some of the whipped topping. Sprinkle one third of the coconut over the topping, pressing it into the topping. Place the second layer over the first and frost the top and sides with the remaining whipped topping.

Sprinkle the remaining coconut evenly over the top and sides of the cake. Serve, or cover loosely and chill until ready to serve.

Note: Go ahead—if you prefer, toast the coconut first to bring out its nutty flavor.

Lane Cake

They'll go coco-nuts over this rich cake that says, "Y'all come back now!"

4 egg whites
1 package (18.25 ounces) white cake mix
1 cup water
¼ cup vegetable oil
1 container (15 ounces) coconut pecan frosting (see Note)
1 jar (10 ounces) maraschino cherries, chopped and well drained
¾ cup coarsely chopped pecans
½ cup raisins, chopped
1 container (16 ounces) white frosting

Preheat the oven to 350°F. In a large bowl, with an electric beater on high speed, beat the egg whites until stiff peaks form. In another large bowl, with the electric beater on medium speed, beat the cake mix, water, and oil for 2 minutes, or until smooth. Fold the beaten egg whites into the cake mixture. Divide the batter between two 9-inch round cake pans that have been coated with nonstick cooking spray. Bake for 20 to 25 minutes, or until a wooden toothpick inserted in the center of each comes out clean. Let cool for 10 minutes, then invert onto wire racks to cool completely. Cut the cake layers in half horizontally, forming 4 layers. In a medium-sized bowl, combine the coconut pecan frosting, cherries, pecans, and raisins; mix well. Place 1 cake layer upside down on a serving plate and frost the top with one third of the coconut mixture. Repeat the layers 2 more times and top with the fourth cake layer. Frost the top and sides with the white frosting. Serve, or cover loosely until ready to serve.

Note: Whether the container says coconut pecan frosting or German chocolate cake frosting, as long as it has coconut and pecans, it's the one to use.

Red Velvet Pound Cake

12 to 16 servings

Sounds like something Scarlett O'Hara would have liked, doesn't it? This elegant-easy dessert is perfect for that special Valentine's Day dessert, or any day that needs a little sweetening up . . . 'cause just one taste will tell everybody how much you really care.

1 package (18.25 ounces) butter-flavored yellow cake mix	3 eggs
	1 bottle (1 ounce) red food color
¼ cup unsweetened cocoa	1½ cups confectioners' sugar
¾ cup (1½ sticks) butter, softened, divided	1 package (8 ounces) cream cheese, softened
1 cup water	1 tablespoon milk

Preheat the oven to 350°F. In a large bowl, with an electric beater on medium speed, beat the cake mix, cocoa, ½ cup butter, the water, and eggs until well mixed. Add the food color and beat until well mixed. Pour the batter into a 10-inch Bundt or tube pan that has been coated with nonstick cooking spray. Bake for 35 to 40 minutes, or until a wooden toothpick inserted in the center comes out clean. Let cool for 15 minutes, then invert onto a wire rack to cool completely. In a medium-sized bowl, with an electric beater on medium speed, beat the confectioners' sugar, cream cheese, milk, and the remaining ¼ cup butter until well mixed and smooth. Frost the cake with the cream cheese frosting. Serve, or cover loosely and chill until ready to serve.

Orange Cake

12 to 16 servings

It's so simple, you'll almost feel guilty calling it homemade. When they keep asking how you made it and where you found the time, just smile and say, "For you, I always have the time!"

1 package (18.25 ounces) yellow cake mix
1 package (4-serving size) orange-flavored gelatin
1 cup vegetable oil
1 cup orange juice
4 eggs

Preheat the oven to 325°F. In a medium-sized bowl, with an electric beater on medium speed, beat all the ingredients for 2 minutes, or until well mixed. Pour the batter into a 10-inch Bundt or tube pan that has been coated with nonstick cooking spray. Bake for 50 to 55 minutes, or until a wooden toothpick inserted in the center comes out clean. Let cool slightly, then invert onto a wire rack to cool completely. Serve, or cover until ready to serve.

Note: Wanna fancy this up a bit? Top it with a glaze made of 1 cup confectioners' sugar mixed with 2 tablespoons orange juice.

Graham Cracker Cake

12 to 15 servings

In the past we've made s'mores with graham crackers, and we've used them for pie shells, too. But that was only a tease for our taste buds. Wait till you try this Alabama graham cracker cake . . . and be sure to have plenty of milk close by!

1½ cups (3 sticks) butter, softened, divided
1½ cups granulated sugar
1 package (13½ ounces) graham cracker crumbs
2 teaspoons baking powder
¾ cup milk
5 eggs
1 teaspoon vanilla extract
½ cup flaked coconut
½ cup chopped pecans
1 box (16 ounces) confectioners' sugar
1 can (8 ounces) crushed pineapple, undrained

Preheat the oven to 350°F. In a large bowl, with an electric beater on medium speed, beat 1 cup butter and the granulated sugar for 3 to 4 minutes, or until creamy. Add the graham cracker crumbs, baking powder, milk, eggs, and vanilla and beat until well mixed. Stir in the coconut and pecans until well mixed. Spread the batter in a 9" × 13" baking pan that has been coated with nonstick cooking spray. In a small bowl, combine the remaining ½ cup butter, the confectioners' sugar, and pineapple until well mixed; pour evenly over the batter. Bake for 45 to 50 minutes, or until a wooden toothpick inserted in the center comes out clean. Allow to cool, then cut and serve, or cover until ready to serve.

Strawberry Cake

12 to 16 servings

Almost every state in the South grows plump juicy strawberries, which means we find them in everything from jams and jellies to pies and, one of my favorites, strawberry cake.

1 package (18.25 ounces) white cake mix	4 eggs
1 package (4-serving size) strawberry-flavored gelatin	⅔ cup vegetable oil
	3 cups confectioners' sugar
	½ cup strawberry preserves
1 package (10 ounces) frozen sweetened sliced strawberries, thawed and drained	⅓ cup butter, softened

Preheat the oven to 350°F. In a large bowl, with an electric beater on medium speed, beat the cake mix, gelatin mix, strawberries, eggs, and oil for 2 to 3 minutes, or until well mixed. Divide the batter between two 9-inch round cake pans that have been coated with nonstick cooking spray. Bake for 30 to 35 minutes, or until a wooden toothpick inserted in the center of each comes out clean. Let cool for 10 minutes, then invert onto wire racks to cool completely. In a medium-sized bowl, with an electric beater on medium speed, beat the confectioners' sugar, strawberry preserves, and butter for 2 to 3 minutes, or until smooth. Place 1 cake layer upside down on a serving plate and frost the top with the strawberry frosting. Place the second layer over the first and frost the top and sides. Chill for 2 hours and then serve, or cover loosely and keep chilled until ready to serve.

Caramel-Nut Cake

12 to 16 servings

Bakery-perfect, home-baked flavor!

1½ cups (3 sticks) butter, softened
2 cups firmly packed light brown sugar
5 eggs
3 cups all-purpose flour
½ teaspoon baking powder
¼ teaspoon salt
½ cup milk
1 teaspoon vanilla extract
2 cups coarsely chopped pecans

Preheat the oven to 325°F. In a large bowl, with an electric beater on medium speed, beat the butter and brown sugar until fluffy. Add the eggs and beat until smooth. Reduce the speed to low and add the flour, baking powder, and salt. Gradually beat in the milk and vanilla until well blended. Stir in the pecans; mix well. Spoon the batter into a 10-inch Bundt or tube pan that has been coated with nonstick cooking spray. Bake for 70 to 75 minutes, or until a wooden toothpick inserted in the center comes out clean. Let cool for 15 minutes, then invert onto a wire rack to cool completely. Serve, or cover until ready to serve.

Bourbon Fruitcake

12 to 16 servings

now the old story that fruitcakes get passed from one per-
the next . . . and no one ever eats them? Well, this one
definitely get eaten—I think it's the bourbon flavor that
kes it so popular!

1 container (16 ounces)
  mixed candied fruit
¼ cup bourbon
1 cup sugar
1 cup (2 sticks) butter,
  softened

5 eggs
2 cups self-rising flour
2 cups coarsely chopped
  walnuts

Preheat the oven to 275°F. In a resealable plastic storage bag, combine the candied fruit and bourbon; let stand for 30 minutes. In a large bowl, with an electric beater on medium speed, beat the sugar, butter, and eggs until creamy. In a medium-sized bowl, combine the flour and walnuts; add to the butter mixture. Add the candied fruit mixture and mix well. Pour the batter into a 10-inch Bundt or tube pan that has been coated with nonstick cooking spray. Bake for 1¾ to 2 hours, or until a wooden toothpick inserted in the center comes out clean. Let cool for 15 minutes, then invert onto a wire rack to cool completely. Serve, or cover until ready to serve.

Easy Peach Cake

12 to 15 servings

Did I tell you this one's a cinch? No need to tell the gang, though—let 'em think you're amazing!

1 package (18.25 ounces) butter-flavored yellow cake mix
¾ cup coarsely chopped pecans

1 container (21 ounces) peach pie filling
⅔ cup vegetable oil
2 eggs
1 teaspoon vanilla extract

Preheat the oven to 350°F. In a large bowl, combine all the ingredients; mix well. Pour the batter into a 9" × 13" baking pan that has been coated with nonstick cooking spray. Bake for 40 to 45 minutes, or until a wooden toothpick inserted in the center comes out clean. Allow to cool slightly and serve warm, or let cool, then cover until ready to serve.

Strawberry Swirl Cake

12 to 16 servings

If looks count, then this one is doubly terrific—pretty on the outside and heavenly tasting throughout!

1 package (18.25 ounces)
   white cake mix
1 cup sour cream
¼ cup water

2 eggs
1 package (4-serving size)
   strawberry-flavored gelatin

Preheat the oven to 350°F. In a medium-sized bowl, with an electric beater on medium speed, beat all the ingredients except the gelatin mix for 2 minutes, or until creamy. Pour one third of the batter into a 10-inch Bundt or tube pan that has been coated with nonstick cooking spray. Sprinkle evenly with half of the gelatin mix. Repeat the layers with the batter and gelatin, then top with the remaining batter. Bake for 45 to 50 minutes, or until a wooden toothpick inserted in the center comes out clean. Let cool for 5 minutes, then invert onto a wire rack to cool completely. Serve, or cover until ready to serve.

Un-Beet-Able Cake

When one of my viewers shared this unusual recipe with me, I have to admit that I thought it was a mistake that there were beets in it. But I gave it a try, and am I glad I did, 'cause it's, well, un-beet-ably moist and tasty!

2½ cups all-purpose flour
2 cups sugar
2 teaspoons baking soda
2 teaspoons ground cinnamon
½ teaspoon salt
1 can (15 ounces) beets, drained and chopped

1 can (8 ounces) crushed pineapple, undrained
1 cup vegetable oil
1 cup cottage cheese
2 eggs
2 teaspoons vanilla extract
¾ cup chopped walnuts

Preheat the oven to 350°F. In a large bowl, with an electric beater on medium speed, beat all the ingredients except the walnuts until well mixed. Stir in the walnuts until well combined. Pour the batter into a 9" × 13" baking pan that has been coated with nonstick cooking spray. Bake for 45 to 50 minutes, or until a wooden toothpick inserted in the center comes out clean. Allow to cool in the pan on a wire rack. Serve, or cover until ready to serve.

Note: Frost with your favorite cream cheese frosting.

Apple Coffee Cake

8 to 10 servings

Don't sit under the apple tree with anything else but this melt-in-your-mouth goody!

1½ cups all-purpose flour
1 cup granulated sugar
1 teaspoon baking powder
½ teaspoon salt
¼ cup (½ stick) butter, melted
1 egg

3 medium-sized apples, peeled, cored, and coarsely chopped
¼ cup firmly packed light brown sugar
½ cup chopped pecans
1 teaspoon ground cinnamon

Preheat the oven to 350°F. In a large bowl, combine the flour, granulated sugar, baking powder, salt, butter, and egg; mix well with a spoon. Stir in the apples. Spread the batter in a 7" × 11" baking dish that has been coated with nonstick cooking spray. In a small bowl, combine the remaining ingredients; mix well and sprinkle evenly over the batter. Bake for 35 to 40 minutes, or until a wooden toothpick inserted in the center comes out clean. Serve warm, or allow to cool and cover until ready to serve.

Note: I like to serve this warm, topped with a scoop of ice cream and some additional pecans sprinkled over the top.

Scotchie Surprise Cupcakes

2 dozen

Put out a basket of these cupcakes, then stand back and watch. . . .
Your gang will really be surprised by the gooey rich filling!

1 package (18.25 ounces) chocolate cake mix, batter prepared according to the package directions
1 package (8 ounces) cream cheese, softened
¼ cup sugar
1 egg
1 cup (6 ounces) butterscotch chips
½ cup chopped walnuts
1 container (16 ounces) cream cheese frosting

Preheat the oven to 350°F. Spoon the prepared batter equally into 24 muffin cups that have been lined with paper baking cups, filling each cup three-quarters full. In a medium-sized bowl, with an electric beater on medium speed, beat the cream cheese, sugar, and egg until fluffy. Stir in the butterscotch chips and walnuts until well mixed. Spoon a heaping teaspoon of the cream cheese mixture into the center of the batter in each cup. Bake for 15 to 20 minutes, or until a wooden toothpick inserted in the cupcakes comes out clean. Allow to cool completely, then frost with the cream cheese frosting. Serve, or cover loosely and refrigerate until ready to serve.

Old-fashioned Pound Cake

12 to 16 servings

The story goes that pound cake got its name because it was originally made with a pound each of most of its ingredients. I've taken a few "pounds" off these ingredients—but the cake still has the same delicious taste that we remember!

3 cups sugar
1 cup (2 sticks) butter,
    softened
½ cup vegetable shortening

5 eggs
3 cups all-purpose flour
1 cup evaporated milk
1 teaspoon vanilla extract

In a large bowl, with an electric beater on medium-high speed, beat the sugar, butter, and shortening until creamy. Add the eggs and beat until fluffy. Add 1½ cups flour and ½ cup evaporated milk, beating until well blended. Add the remaining 1½ cups flour and ½ cup evaporated milk and the vanilla, beating until well mixed. Pour the batter into a 10-inch Bundt or tube pan that has been coated with nonstick cooking spray and lightly floured. Place in a cold oven and bake at 300°F. for 1¾ to 2 hours, or until a wooden toothpick inserted in the center comes out clean. Let cool for 10 minutes, then invert onto a wire rack to cool completely. Serve, or cover until ready to serve.

Note: For breakfast, take a few slices and pop them in the toaster. Spread the toasted slices with honey butter—which is no more than a stick of softened butter flavored with a couple tablespoons of honey. Or frost with Vanilla Butter Frosting (page 278).

Vanilla Butter Frosting

about 1 cup

I fashioned this one after a frosting I found topping cupcakes at a school bake sale. The rich buttery taste says this is certainly homemade and ready for topping almost anything.

1½ cups confectioners' sugar
¼ cup (½ stick) butter,
   softened

¼ cup vegetable shortening
1 tablespoon milk
½ teaspoon vanilla extract

In a large bowl, with an electric beater on medium-low speed, beat all the ingredients for 3 to 4 minutes, or until creamy. Use immediately, or cover and chill until ready to use. Bring to room temperature before using.

Note: Perfect to frost Old-fashioned Pound Cake or most plain cakes baked in a 9" × 13" pan. To frost a layer cake, double the quantity of the ingredients and make a double batch.

Sweet Treats
Pies, Puddings, Cookies, and Candies

continued

Lemon Chess Pie

This is a tart lemon filling sandwiched between two crusts. Know what makes it extraordinary? The top crust forms while it's baking!

2 cups sugar
4 eggs
¼ cup (½ stick) butter, melted
¼ cup milk
2 tablespoons yellow cornmeal
2 tablespoons lemon juice

1 tablespoon all-purpose flour
1 tablespoon grated lemon peel
One 9-inch frozen ready-to-bake deep-dish pie shell, thawed

Preheat the oven to 350°F. In a large bowl, with an electric beater on medium speed, beat all the ingredients except the pie shell for 1 to 2 minutes, or until well mixed. Pour into the pie shell and bake for 45 to 50 minutes, or until a crust forms on top and turns golden. Serve warm, or let cool, cover, and chill until ready to serve.

Note: The pie will be a little loose when it comes out of the oven, so if you'd rather have nice, neat pieces of pie, allow it to cool, then chill it for about 4 hours to firm up.

Polka Dot Peach Pie

6 to 8 servings

There's nothing quite like the taste of fresh peaches, and with this easy-as-pie crust that's decorated with a polka dot design, peach pie will surely be tops on your list!

5 large ripe peaches, peeled
   and sliced (see Note)
½ cup sugar
¼ cup all-purpose flour
3 tablespoons butter, melted

1 teaspoon vanilla extract
1 package (15 ounces) folded
   refrigerated pie crust
   (2 crusts)

Preheat the oven to 375°F. In a large bowl, combine all the ingredients except the pie crust; mix well. Unfold one pie crust and place in a 9-inch pie plate, pressing the crust firmly into the plate.

Spoon the peach mixture into the crust. Place the remaining pie crust on a work surface and, using a 1-inch round cookie cutter, cut fifteen circles from the center, forming polka dots, leaving a 1-inch border around the edge (see Note). Place the crust over the peach mixture. Pinch together and trim the edges to seal, then flute, if desired. Bake for 35 to 40 minutes, or until the crust is golden and the filling is bubbly. Let cool before serving.

Note: If fresh peaches aren't in season or available, you can use a 16-ounce package of frozen sliced peaches in place of the fresh. And, if you'd like, 8 to 10 of the round cut-outs can be stirred into the filling before spooning it into the crust. This forms little "dumplings" as the pie cooks, giving it a real Southern cobbler taste. If you don't have a 1-inch cookie cutter, the plastic cap of a soda bottle is the right size—and it works great.

Strawberry Pie

6 to 8 servings

Only one thing sounds better than picking strawberries early in the morning—that's rushing home to make a pie in the afternoon so we can eat a big slice under the shade tree in the backyard.

One 9-inch frozen ready-to-bake deep-dish pie shell, thawed	½ cup sugar
	3 tablespoons cornstarch
	¾ cup ginger ale
1 package (4-serving size) strawberry-flavored gelatin	1 quart fresh strawberries, hulled and cut in half

Bake the pie shell according to the package directions; set aside to cool. In a medium-sized saucepan, combine the remaining ingredients except the strawberries over medium heat. Cook for 5 to 7 minutes, or until the gelatin has dissolved and the mixture is clear, stirring occasionally. Remove from the heat and let cool for about 5 minutes. Stir in the strawberries and pour into the baked pie shell. Chill for at least 4 hours, or until set. Serve, or cover and keep chilled until ready to serve.

Note: Before serving, why not top each slice with a dollop of whipped topping and a whole strawberry?

Fruit Pockets

Warm and wonderful! What a perfect way to enjoy the fruity taste of summer . . . anytime!

1 large package (17.3 ounces) refrigerated buttermilk biscuits (8 biscuits)
2 containers (20 ounces each) peach pie filling, drained (see Note)

¼ teaspoon ground cinnamon
½ cup (1 stick) butter, melted

Preheat the oven to 350°F. Flour a work surface and rolling pin. Roll each biscuit into a 6-inch circle. In a medium-sized bowl, combine the pie filling and cinnamon; mix well. Divide the filling equally among the dough circles, forming a semicircle of filling on half of each circle and leaving a ½-inch border around the edge. Fold the dough over the filling, forming half-moons. With your fingers or a fork, pinch or press the edges together firmly to seal. Place the pockets on 2 large rimmed baking sheets that have been coated with 2 tablespoons melted butter each. Brush the remaining butter evenly over the tops of the pockets. Bake for 15 minutes, then turn the pockets over and bake for 5 to 7 more minutes, or until golden. Serve warm, or let cool before serving.

Note: Any flavor pie filling can be used, but besides peach my other favorites are apple and blueberry.

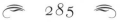

Watermelon Pie

6 to 8 servings

Take along one or two of these to your next family backyard get-together—for a cool, refreshing change-of-pace pie.

1 can (14 ounces) sweetened condensed milk
¼ cup lemon juice
1 container (8 ounces) frozen whipped topping, thawed
2 cups cubed and seeded watermelon, well drained
One 9-inch graham cracker pie crust

In a large bowl, beat together the sweetened condensed milk and lemon juice until thick. Add the whipped topping and mix until thoroughly combined. Add the watermelon; mix well. Spoon into the pie crust, cover, and chill for at least 4 hours, or until ready to serve.

Note: How juicy and ripe the watermelon is will determine how firm the pie comes out. Just make sure to drain the watermelon well, and if the pie slices are a little loose, it's okay, 'cause it still tastes good.

Golden Blueberry Crumb Cobbler

6 to 8 servings

Served plain or with a scoop of vanilla ice cream, this hot and bubbly treat will chase your "blues" away!

1½ pints fresh blueberries
5 tablespoons butter,
   softened, divided

1½ cups sugar
1¼ cups all-purpose flour

Preheat the oven to 350°F. Place the blueberries in a 7" × 11" baking dish that has been coated with 1 tablespoon butter. In a medium-sized bowl, combine the remaining 4 tablespoons butter, the sugar, and flour; mix well until crumbly. Sprinkle the flour mixture evenly over the blueberries. Bake for 40 to 45 minutes, or until the topping is golden and the blueberries are bubbly. Serve warm, or allow to cool before serving.

Sunny Lemon Pie

6 to 8 servings

Sure to be a hit, this one's certainly no "lemon" in my book. One taste will have them begging for seconds!

1 package (4-serving size) lemon pie filling, cooked according to the package directions
¼ cup (½ stick) butter
2 tablespoons lemon juice
1½ teaspoons grated lemon peel

1 cup sour cream
One 9-inch graham cracker pie crust
2 cups frozen whipped topping, thawed

While the lemon pie filling is still hot, add the butter, lemon juice, and lemon peel; stir until the butter is melted. Let cool, then add the sour cream; mix well. Pour the mixture into the pie crust and chill for at least 2 hours, or until set. Completely cover the top of the pie with the whipped topping and serve, or cover loosely and chill until ready to serve.

Note: Wanna add a little more pucker power to each bite? Simply top the pie with grated lemon peel just before serving.

Scrumptious Coconut Pie

6 to 8 servings

Long ago, coconuts were used as ballast to equalize the weight load on ships headed for our Southern shores. Once the ships landed, the coconuts were put to good use in many recipes, like this scrumptious pie!

One 9-inch frozen ready-to-bake pie shell, thawed
2 cups milk
3 eggs
1 cup flaked coconut
½ cup sugar
6 tablespoons all-purpose flour
1 tablespoon butter, softened
1 teaspoon vanilla extract
⅛ teaspoon salt

Bake the pie shell according to the package directions; set aside to cool. In a medium-sized saucepan, whisk together the remaining ingredients. Cook over medium heat for 5 to 7 minutes, or until thickened. Pour into the baked pie shell and chill for at least 4 hours, or until set. Serve, or cover and keep chilled until ready to serve.

Note: We can sprinkle this with ¼ cup toasted coconut to give it a golden-topped finish.

Watermelon Rind Pie

6 to 8 servings

Southerners sure love food—and they hate to see it go to waste. That's why they make this pie that uses the rind of the watermelon. I have to say that from the taste, you'd never know the pie was made with the part of the fruit we usually throw away!

2 containers (10 ounces each) watermelon rind pickles, drained and coarsely chopped (see Note)
½ cup raisins
½ cup chopped pecans

2 teaspoons all-purpose flour
1 teaspoon ground cinnamon
1 package (15 ounces) folded refrigerated pie crust (2 crusts)

Preheat the oven to 350°F. In a medium-sized bowl, combine all the ingredients except the pie crust; mix well. Unfold 1 pie crust and place in a 9-inch pie plate, pressing the crust firmly against the plate. Spoon the watermelon rind mixture into the pie crust, then place the remaining pie crust over the mixture. Trim and pinch the edges together to seal, then flute, if desired. Using a sharp knife, cut four 1-inch slits in the top. Bake for 40 to 45 minutes, or until the crust is golden. Serve warm, or allow to cool before serving.

Note: Check out how to make your own watermelon rind pickles on page 28. You'll need about 2 cups for this recipe.

Perfect Pecan Pie

Yup, it's the real thing—the one you've been waiting for. And boy, oh boy, was it ever worth the wait!

1 cup light corn syrup
3 tablespoons butter
½ cup firmly packed light brown sugar
2 tablespoons all-purpose flour
¼ teaspoon salt

3 eggs, lightly beaten
1½ teaspoons vanilla extract
1½ cups coarsely chopped pecans
One 9-inch frozen ready-to-bake deep-dish pie shell, thawed

Preheat the oven to 350°F. In a large saucepan, combine the corn syrup, butter, brown sugar, flour, and salt over medium heat; stir until the butter melts. Remove from the heat and let cool slightly; add the eggs and vanilla and mix well. Stir in the pecans and pour into the pie shell. Bake for 55 to 60 minutes, or until firm. Serve warm or allow to cool before serving.

Chocolate Cream Cheese Pie

6 to 8 servings

You'll want to have the gang over just to show off this luscious Southern "quickie"!

One 9-inch frozen ready-to-bake pie shell, thawed
1 package (8 ounces) cream cheese, softened
1 package (4-serving size) instant chocolate pudding and pie filling

1½ cups cold milk
1 cup frozen whipped topping, thawed

Bake the pie shell according to the package directions; set aside to cool. In a large bowl, with an electric beater on medium speed, beat the cream cheese until smooth. Add the chocolate pudding mix and milk and beat until well combined. Pour into the pie shell and top with the whipped topping. Cover and chill for at least 2 hours before serving.

Note: For that fancy bakery look, garnish with shaved chocolate, chocolate sprinkles, or any other favorite topping.

Sweet Potato Custard Pie

6 to 8 servings

This is a super holiday pie, but once you've tried it, you may find yourself making any day a holiday!

1 can (29 ounces) sweet potatoes or yams, drained
1 can (14 ounces) sweetened condensed milk
2 eggs

¼ teaspoon ground nutmeg
One 9-inch frozen ready-to-bake deep-dish pie shell, thawed

Preheat the oven to 350°F. In a large bowl, combine all the ingredients except the pie shell. Beat with an electric beater on medium speed until smooth and well mixed. Pour into the pie shell and bake for 55 to 60 minutes, or until the center is set. Allow to cool slightly and serve warm, or cool, then cover and chill until ready to serve.

Double-Crusted Custard Pie

With all the dairy farms there are down South, it's no wonder so many recipes are filled to the brim with creamy goodness! And, top to bottom, this one is pure eating pleasure.

3 eggs	2 tablespoons white vinegar
1½ cups sugar	1 tablespoon vanilla extract
¼ cup (½ stick) butter, melted	One 9-inch frozen ready-to-bake deep-dish pie shell, thawed
2 tablespoons all-purpose flour	

Preheat the oven to 300°F. In a medium-sized bowl, with an electric beater on medium speed, beat the eggs until fluffy. Add the sugar, butter, and flour and continue beating until well combined. Stir in the vinegar and vanilla; mix well. Pour into the pie shell and bake for 60 to 70 minutes, or until a crust forms on top and turns golden. Serve warm, or allow to cool, then cover and chill until ready to serve.

Egg Custard

Get crackin' and make up a creamy-smooth pie that would make any Southern belle proud!

¾ cup sugar
3 tablespoons all-purpose
  flour
3 eggs

1 can (12 ounces) evaporated
  milk
2 tablespoons butter, melted
1 tablespoon vanilla extract

Preheat the oven to 350°F. In a medium-sized bowl, combine the sugar, flour, and eggs; mix well. Add the remaining ingredients; mix well. Pour into a 9-inch pie plate that has been coated with nonstick cooking spray. Bake for 35 to 40 minutes, or until the center is firm. Let cool slightly and serve warm, or allow to cool, then cover and chill until ready to serve.

Note: If you want to make an egg custard pie, pour the custard filling into a thawed 9-inch frozen ready-to-bake deep-dish pie crust and proceed as directed above.

My Own Pie Crust

The secret to every successful pie is the great crust—and now you've got your very own to start with!

1½ cups all-purpose flour
3 tablespoons sugar
1 teaspoon salt

½ cup vegetable oil
2 tablespoons cold milk

If planning to use this as a prebaked shell, preheat the oven to 425°F. In a 9-inch pie plate, combine the flour, sugar, and salt. In a small bowl, whisk together the oil and milk and pour over the flour mixture. Using a fork, mix until the dry ingredients are completely moistened. Using your fingers, press the dough evenly over the bottom and up the sides of the plate, partly covering the rim. To use as a prebaked shell, prick the dough all over with a fork and bake for 12 to 15 minutes, or until set, then cool and fill as desired. To use as an unbaked shell, fill with the desired pie filling and bake according to the pie filling directions.

Note: This is a cookie-like shortbread-style crust, so you're in for a real treat!

Tipsy Pudding

8 to 10 servings

With a name like this, there's no doubt that this pudding has a little something extra to give it a "kick." One taste of this very grown-up pudding, and you'll be back for more! (But keep this one for grown-ups only, please!)

3 cups cold milk
1 package (4-serving size) instant vanilla pudding and pie filling
2 cups (1 pint) heavy cream
6 tablespoons confectioners' sugar

One 10-inch angel food cake, cut into 1½-inch chunks
⅓ cup cream sherry
½ cup sliced almonds

In a medium-sized bowl, whisk the milk and pudding mix for 1 to 2 minutes, or until well combined. In a large bowl, with an electric beater on high speed, beat the heavy cream and confectioners' sugar until stiff peaks form. Place half the cake chunks in the bottom of a large glass serving bowl or trifle dish. Sprinkle with half of the sherry, then cover with half of the pudding mixture and half of the whipped cream mixture. Repeat the layers once more, then top with the almonds. Cover loosely and chill for at least 2 hours before serving.

Bread Custard Pudding

6 to 8 servings

If you believe that the way to their hearts is through their stomachs, serve this along with a glass of cold milk or maybe some refreshing iced tea. You should enjoy this one while relaxing with the ones you love best!

3 slices white bread, torn into
   1-inch pieces
2½ cups milk
4 eggs
½ cup granulated sugar

3 tablespoons butter, melted
½ teaspoon salt
2 tablespoons confectioners'
   sugar

Preheat the oven to 350°F. Place the bread in a 1½-quart casserole dish that has been coated with nonstick cooking spray; set aside. In a large bowl, combine the milk, eggs, granulated sugar, butter, and salt; mix well. Pour over the bread and let sit for 5 minutes, or until the liquid is absorbed by the bread. Place the casserole dish in a large baking pan of hot water, with just enough water to go halfway up the sides of the casserole dish. Bake for 80 to 90 minutes, or until the top is set and golden. Carefully remove from the hot water bath and allow to cool for about 20 minutes. Then cover and chill for at least 3 hours before serving. When ready to serve, sprinkle with the confectioners' sugar.

Banana Pudding Parfait

This is kind of like the English trifle of the South.

1 package (12 ounces) vanilla
  wafer cookies
4 large ripe bananas, cut into
  ¼-inch slices
3¼ cups cold milk

1 package (4-serving size)
  instant vanilla pudding
  and pie filling
1 teaspoon vanilla extract

In a 2-quart glass serving bowl, alternately layer the cookies and banana slices, ending with the cookies. In a large bowl, whisk the milk, pudding mix, and vanilla until smooth. Pour over the wafers and bananas. Cover and chill for at least 2 hours before serving.

Note: Assemble this in tall stemmed glasses and make your dessert look extraordinary!

Boiled Custard

about 1 quart

Boiled custard is the basis of so many Southern desserts. Whether we pour it over pieces of cake, use it as the custard in our banana pie, or simply drizzle it over fruit, you'll love the light, rich flavor. And, yes, I said drizzle or pour . . . 'cause this is a thin custard, almost like a sauce.

4 cups (1 quart) milk	3 eggs
1 cup sugar	1 tablespoon vanilla extract

In a large saucepan, combine the milk, sugar, and eggs. Cook over medium heat for 12 to 15 minutes, or until the mixture bubbles, whisking frequently. Whisk constantly for 5 to 6 more minutes, until it coats a spoon and is shiny. Whisk in the vanilla and remove from the heat. Let cool slightly before using.

Note: Do not overcook this, or the eggs will cause it to curdle. Sometimes I like to serve it over gelatin cubes. You can even freeze it and serve as frozen custard.

Ambrosia

Serve this up in a clear glass bowl for a colorful, refreshing salad or light, fresh-tasting dessert.

6 oranges

1 cup flaked coconut

6 maraschino cherries,
   halved and drained

Over a medium-sized bowl, peel and section the oranges, allowing the juice and sections to fall into the bowl. Add the coconut and cherries to the orange sections; mix well. Cover and chill for at least 1 hour, or until ready to serve.

Note: Traditionally, ambrosia is this simple, but I've seen it made with pineapple chunks and miniature marshmallows, too. Try it either way.

Cream-Coated Grapes

4 to 6 servings

These grapes are really dressed up! The sour cream coating makes them elegant enough to eat with a spoon.

1 cup sour cream (see Note)
½ cup firmly packed light
   brown sugar

1 pound seedless green
   grapes, washed, drained,
   and stemmed

In a large bowl, combine the sour cream and brown sugar, stirring until the sugar has dissolved. Add the grapes; mix well. Spoon into parfait glasses, bowls, or even champagne glasses, cover, and chill for at least 2 hours before serving.

Note: A lighter alternative is to use plain yogurt in place of the sour cream.

Pecan Sandies

about 4 dozen

These are the kind of sandies that we grew up with—well, almost. I think this is one of the best versions I've ever tasted. If you like a simple, not-too-sweet cookie, put this on your list of favorites.

1 cup (2 sticks) butter, softened	2 teaspoons vanilla extract
¼ cup confectioners' sugar	2 cups all-purpose flour
	1 cup chopped pecans

Preheat the oven to 325°F. In a large bowl, with an electric beater on medium speed, cream the butter and confectioners' sugar for 1 minute. Add the vanilla; mix well. With a spoon, stir in the flour and pecans. Drop by teaspoonfuls about 1 inch apart onto ungreased baking sheets. Bake for 12 to 15 minutes, or until the edges are golden; do not overbake. Let cool before serving.

Note: Dust the tops of these with a bit of confectioners' sugar right before serving.

Swedish Wedding Cookies

What a perfect marriage—melt-in-your-mouth morsels that go with any festive occasion!

1 cup (2 sticks) butter, softened	2 teaspoons water
⅓ cup granulated sugar	2 cups all-purpose flour
2 teaspoons vanilla extract	1 cup finely chopped pecans
	½ cup confectioners' sugar

Preheat the oven to 325°F. In a large bowl, with an electric beater on medium speed, cream the butter and granulated sugar until fluffy. Add the vanilla and water and beat well. With a spoon, stir in the flour and pecans. Shape into 1-inch balls and place about 1 inch apart on ungreased cookie sheets. Bake for 20 to 25 minutes, or until the bottoms of the cookies are light golden. Remove to wire racks to cool completely. Place the confectioners' sugar in a resealable plastic storage bag; add a few cookies at a time and shake until completely coated. Store in an airtight container until ready to serve.

Note: Perfect to make ahead and have on hand for drop-in company, these'll stay fresh for a couple of weeks if stored properly.

Cookie-Jar Tea Cakes

about 4 dozen

A long-lasting tea cake is a hard cookie that's perfect for the cookie jar!

1 cup granulated sugar
½ cup (1 stick) butter, softened
1 egg
½ teaspoon vanilla extract
2½ cups all-purpose flour

½ teaspoon baking soda
Confectioners' sugar
1 package (12 ounces) semisweet chocolate chips, melted

Preheat the oven to 350°F. In a large bowl, with an electric beater on medium speed, cream the granulated sugar and butter until fluffy. Add the egg and vanilla, beating well. With a spoon, stir in the flour and baking soda; the dough will be dry and crumbly. Using your hands, work the dough for 4 to 5 minutes, or until a smooth, stiff dough forms. Lightly dust a work surface with confectioners' sugar. Using a rolling pin, roll the dough to a ⅛-inch thickness. Using a 2-inch round cookie cutter, cut out cookies and place 1 inch apart on ungreased cookie sheets. Bake for 10 to 12 minutes, or until golden. Allow to cool slightly, then remove to wire racks to cool completely. Turn half of the cookies over and spread the flat sides with the melted chocolate. Top each with another cookie, forming sandwiches. Allow the chocolate to cool completely, until set. Serve, or store in an airtight container until ready to serve.

continued

Note: Remember to roll out the cookies nice and thin. Then they'll get nice and crisp when baking. And if there's some left-over chocolate, drizzle it over the finished cookies to give them an even fancier look.

Holiday Cherry-Nut Logs

4 logs; 4 dozen slices

These make edible holiday gift treats that "yule" love . . . and so will your gang! (You know, these are yummy for any time of the year!)

1 package (12 ounces) vanilla wafer cookies, crushed
2 cups chopped pecans
2 cups raisins
1½ cups miniature marshmallows

1 jar (6 ounces) maraschino cherries, drained and chopped
1 can (14 ounces) sweetened condensed milk
¼ cup confectioners' sugar

In a large bowl, combine all the ingredients except the confectioners' sugar; mix well. Form the mixture into 4 logs about 1½" × 6". Place the confectioners' sugar in a shallow dish and roll the logs in the sugar, coating completely. Wrap each log in plastic wrap and chill for at least 4 hours, or until firm. Slice just before serving.

Note: Make colorful holiday gifts by wrapping these logs in colored plastic wrap or cellophane and tying with ribbons.

Crunchy Cinnamon Crisps

4 dozen

Need something sweet and quick for drop-ins? Somewhere between a cookie and candy, these are the answer!

24 whole cinnamon graham crackers

1 cup firmly packed light brown sugar

1 cup (2 sticks) butter

1½ cups chopped pecans

Preheat the oven to 300°F. Line 2 rimmed baking sheets with aluminum foil. Place the graham crackers on the baking sheets in a single layer. In a medium-sized saucepan, bring the brown sugar and butter to a boil over medium-low heat, stirring frequently. Allow to boil for 5 to 6 minutes, or until the sugar is dissolved, stirring constantly. Stir in the pecans and remove from the heat. Pour over the graham crackers, coating completely. Bake for 10 minutes, then remove from the oven and allow to cool. Break the cookies in half and store in an airtight container until ready to serve.

Note: Make sure not to store these in the refrigerator, or they'll become soft and grainy.

Pecan Tassies

2 dozen

These little mini-tarts with a cream cheese crust are a common treat in the Deep South. A favorite of President Clinton's, they'll surely please your gang—no matter what party you're having!

½ cup (1 stick) plus
   1 tablespoon butter,
   softened, divided
1 package (3 ounces) cream
   cheese, softened
1 cup all-purpose flour

½ cup firmly packed light
   brown sugar
1 egg
1 teaspoon vanilla extract
⅛ teaspoon salt
½ cup chopped pecans

In a large bowl, with an electric beater on medium speed, beat ½ cup butter and the cream cheese until creamy. Add the flour, beating until well combined. Cover and chill the dough for 30 minutes. Preheat the oven to 325°F. In another large bowl, combine the remaining ingredients, including the remaining 1 tablespoon butter; stir until well combined. Shape the chilled dough into twenty-four 1-inch balls. Place each dough ball in an ungreased mini-muffin cup. Using your thumb, press the dough to form a crust. Spoon the pecan mixture into the crusts, filling them three-quarters full. Bake for 35 to 40 minutes, or until the filling is firm and the crust is golden. Cool slightly, then remove to a wire rack to cool completely. Serve, or cover and chill until ready to serve.

Buttery Sticky Roll-ups

6 servings

The whole gang'll be stuck on these super-easy snack-time treats!

1 cup sugar
¼ cup (½ stick) butter, melted
1 tablespoon vanilla extract

1 package (8 ounces) refrigerated crescent rolls
¼ cup water

Preheat the oven to 375°F. In a medium-sized bowl, combine the sugar, butter, and vanilla; mix well and set aside. Unroll the crescent rolls and press the seams together to form one large rectangle. Spread the sugar mixture evenly over the dough and roll up jelly-roll style from a long side. Cut into 6 equal slices and place cut side down in a 9" × 5" loaf pan that has been coated with nonstick cooking spray. Pour the water into the pan and bake for 30 to 35 minutes, or until golden on top. Remove from the oven and let cool slightly. Serve warm.

Note: This is one of those things that you have to bake and then eat right away. It's best fresh from the oven.

Pineapple Fritters

about 2 dozen

Fritters are simply small amounts of yummy batter that are deep-fried. These are especially tasty 'cause they're overflowing with the flavor of juicy pineapple.

3 cups all-purpose flour
1 can (20 ounces) crushed
   pineapple, drained
1 cup milk
1 egg
3 tablespoons granulated
   sugar

2 tablespoons butter, melted
2½ teaspoons baking powder
1 cup vegetable oil
1 cup confectioners' sugar

In a large bowl, combine all the ingredients except the oil and confectioners' sugar; mix well. In a large skillet, heat the oil over medium heat until hot but not smoking. Drop the pineapple mixture by heaping tablespoonfuls, a few at a time, into the skillet. Cook for 1 to 2 minutes per side, until golden on both sides. Drain on a paper towel–lined platter. Place the confectioners' sugar in a shallow dish. Carefully dip the hot fritters in the sugar, coating completely. Serve immediately.

Marbled Brownie Bars

12 to 15 bars

These are a festive addition to any dessert table. They're sure to bring smiles . . . and shouts for more!

2 packages (8 ounces each) cream cheese, softened
2 eggs
2 tablespoons sugar
1 teaspoon vanilla extract

1 package (21 ounces) brownie mix, batter prepared according to the package directions

Preheat the oven to 350°F. In a medium-sized bowl, with an electric beater on medium speed, beat the cream cheese, eggs, sugar, and vanilla until fluffy. Spread half of the brownie batter in a 9" × 13" baking pan that has been coated with nonstick baking spray. Spoon the cream cheese mixture over the brownie batter, then top with the remaining brownie batter. Using a table knife, cut through the batter, swirling to create a marbled effect. Bake for 35 to 40 minutes, or until a wooden toothpick inserted in the center comes out clean. Allow to cool, then cut into bars and serve, or cover and chill until ready to serve.

Butter Pecan Fudge

about 5 dozen pieces

Craving something sweet? Nothing satisfies like thick, creamy fudge. And Southern-style butter pecan fudge is the cream of the crop!

½ cup (1 stick) butter
½ cup heavy cream
½ cup granulated sugar
½ cup firmly packed light
   brown sugar

⅛ teaspoon salt
1 cup pecan halves, toasted
1 teaspoon vanilla extract
2 cups confectioners' sugar

In a large saucepan, bring the butter, heavy cream, granulated sugar, brown sugar, and salt to a boil over medium heat, stirring frequently. Allow to boil for 5 minutes, stirring constantly. Remove from the heat and stir in the pecans and vanilla. Add the confectioners' sugar and stir until smooth and well combined. Spread into an 8-inch square baking dish that has been coated with nonstick cooking spray. Freeze for 25 to 30 minutes, or until firm. Cut into 1-inch squares and serve, or store in an airtight container until ready to serve.

Old-fashioned Peanut Brittle

about 1 pound

This old-fashioned family favorite is sure to bring plenty of smiles!

2 tablespoons butter,
  softened
1½ cups sugar
½ cup light corn syrup
2 tablespoons water

¼ teaspoon salt
1½ cups unsalted dry-roasted
  peanuts
1 teaspoon baking soda

Line a large rimmed baking sheet with aluminum foil and grease the foil with the butter. In a large saucepan, bring the sugar, corn syrup, water, and salt to a boil over high heat. Add the peanuts and continue cooking until the sugar syrup is golden and the hard ball stage is reached, stirring constantly (see Note). Remove from the heat and stir in the baking soda. Spread the peanut mixture in a thin layer on the prepared baking sheet and allow to cool completely. Break into bite-sized pieces and serve, or store in an airtight container until ready to serve.

Note: To test for the hard ball stage: Drop a bit of the mixture from a teaspoon into a glass of cold water. If it forms a ball and remains a ball when it touches the bottom of the glass, it has reached the hard ball stage. If not, continue to cook the mixture, then test it again after a bit. Oh—be careful when working with the hot sugar mixture!

Chocolate Pralines

about 3 dozen

Pralines are a rich, patty-shaped Southern candy made from pecans. And for all you chocoholics out there, these are "to die for"!

¼ cup (½ stick) plus 1 teaspoon butter, divided
2½ cups sugar
1 cup buttermilk
½ teaspoon baking soda

1 teaspoon salt
½ cup semisweet chocolate chips
1 teaspoon vanilla extract
2 cups pecan halves

In a large saucepan that has been coated with 1 teaspoon butter, combine the sugar, buttermilk, baking soda, and salt. Bring to a boil over high heat. Reduce the heat to medium and cook for about 20 minutes, until the soft ball stage is reached, stirring constantly (see Note). Remove from the heat and add the remaining ¼ cup butter, the chocolate chips, and vanilla; continue stirring until the butter and chocolate are melted and smooth. Add the pecans and stir until well coated. Drop by tablespoonfuls about 1 inch apart onto waxed paper–lined baking sheets. Allow to cool at room temperature until set. Store in an airtight container until ready to serve.

Note: To test for the soft ball stage: Drop a bit of the mixture from a teaspoon into a glass of cold water. If it forms a soft ball that flattens when you remove it from the water, it has reached the soft ball stage. If not, continue to cook the mixture, then test again after a bit.

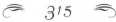

Butter Mints

about 5 dozen

Southerners just love mint. Why, down South, mint leaves are often found wreathing the front porch of farm and plantation houses. So it stands to reason that there are plenty of ways to use them. You'll find these mints, made from mint extract, gracing the buffet tables of many a wedding or other festive occasion!

1 box (16 ounces)
   confectioners' sugar
½ cup (1 stick) butter,
   softened

5 teaspoons heavy cream
¼ teaspoon mint extract
2 drops green food color

In a medium-sized bowl, with an electric beater on medium speed, beat the sugar and butter for 2 to 3 minutes, until creamy. Add the cream, mint extract, and food color and continue beating for 3 to 4 minutes, until well blended. Roll into ½-inch balls. Using your thumb, lightly push down the center of each ball to form a wafer; place on a wire rack and allow to dry, uncovered, overnight. Transfer to an airtight container until ready to serve.

Chocolate Pecan Fudge

about 5 dozen pieces

Wanna make fabulous foolproof fudge? Follow these easy steps!

1 can (5 ounces) evaporated milk
1⅔ cups sugar
½ teaspoon salt
2 cups miniature marshmallows

1½ cups (9 ounces) semisweet chocolate chips
1 cup chopped pecans
1 teaspoon vanilla extract

In a large saucepan, combine the evaporated milk, sugar, and salt over low heat. Bring to a boil and allow to boil for 5 minutes, stirring constantly. Remove from the heat and add the remaining ingredients, stirring until the marshmallows and chocolate chips are melted. Pour into an 8-inch square baking dish that has been coated with nonstick cooking spray. Allow to cool until firm, then cut into 1-inch squares. Serve, or store in an airtight container until ready to serve.

Southern Sippers
Drinks, Punches, and Toddies

Country Lemonade

about 1½ quarts; 4 to 6 servings

One sip of this fresh-squeezed lemonade and you'll know exactly why it's a top choice with everything from zippy barbecue to the most delicate finger foods.

¾ cup sugar
1 cup hot water
4 cups cold water

½ cup fresh lemon juice
   (see Note)
1 lemon, thinly sliced

In a pitcher, combine the sugar and hot water, stirring until the sugar has dissolved. Add the cold water, lemon juice, and lemon slices; mix well. Serve, or chill until ready to serve.

Note: Depending on the size, 4 to 5 lemons should produce about ½ cup fresh juice. When you're ready to serve this, bring out a big glass pitcher and serve it over ice, garnished with additional lemon slices and some fresh mint leaves.

Russian Tea

about 1 gallon; 12 to 16 servings

Okay, pinkies up—those teacups are filled with zippy Southern sunshine that'll surely make it a hot item at your house.

6 cups water
¾ cup sugar
6 tea bags
1 lemon, thinly sliced

6 cups orange juice
1 can (46 ounces) pineapple
  juice

In a large pot, combine the water, sugar, tea bags, and lemon; bring to a boil over medium-high heat and allow to boil for 2 minutes. Remove and discard the tea bags. Add the orange juice and pineapple juice and return to a boil. Serve hot in individual cups or glasses.

Note: Garnish each serving with an orange slice or a wedge of fresh pineapple.

Hot Spiced Cider

about 1 gallon; 12 to 16 servings

This isn't much different from the hot cider I grew up on in the chilly Northeast. I guess that proves that it's an all-American drink!

1 gallon apple cider
1 orange, sliced
½ cup firmly packed light
    brown sugar

3 cinnamon sticks
1 tablespoon whole cloves

In a large pot, bring all the ingredients to a boil over medium-high heat. Reduce the heat to low and simmer for 10 minutes. Serve hot.

Note: This is great made in and served from a slow cooker. Not only does it stay hot and ready to serve, but it also fills the house with a great aroma.

Perky Cinnamon Water

So simple, you'll wish you'd thought of this before. What a neat way to perk up plain water!

5 cups water
½ cup sugar
2 cinnamon sticks

1 whole clove
Ice cubes

In a large saucepan, bring all the ingredients except the ice to a boil over high heat. Remove from the heat, cover, and allow to cool. Discard the cinnamon sticks and clove. Serve in individual glasses over ice.

Simply Refreshing Iced Tea

about 1 gallon; 12 to 16 servings

What could taste better on a lazy, hot afternoon?!

12 cups water
1½ cups sugar

7 tea bags
8 cups ice cubes

In a large saucepan, combine the water, sugar, and tea bags and bring to a boil over high heat; allow to boil for 2 minutes, stirring occasionally. Remove and discard the tea bags. Transfer to a 1-gallon container and add the ice, stirring to cool the mixture. Serve immediately in individual glasses over additional ice, or chill until ready to serve.

Note: The best container to use for making iced tea is one of those gallon containers with the spout at the bottom for serving it. You might like to do what I do and squeeze a wedge of lemon, lime, or orange into each serving right before serving.

Sparkling Banana Punch

about 1 gallon; 12 to 16 servings

This one's often seen at outdoor wedding rehearsal dinners in the South. So gather 'round the punch bowl for good taste and good times!

1 can (6 ounces) frozen orange juice concentrate, thawed
1 can (6 ounces) pineapple juice

1 tablespoon lemon juice
2 medium-sized ripe bananas
1 cup sugar
2 cups water
2 liters ginger ale, chilled

In a blender, blend the orange juice concentrate, pineapple juice, lemon juice, bananas, and sugar on high speed until the bananas are puréed and the mixture is thoroughly blended. Add the water and blend well. Pour into a 9" × 13" baking dish, cover, and freeze for 2 hours, or until the mixture has frozen 1 inch in from the sides of the dish. Remove from the freezer and mix well, being sure to blend the ice crystals with the remaining mixture. Transfer to a punch bowl and add the ginger ale, stirring carefully.

Note: This can also be made ahead of time by preparing the juice mixture and allowing it to freeze completely. Just remove it from the freezer 1 hour before serving and stir it to a slushy consistency. Combine with the ginger ale as above.

Grapevine Punch

about 1 gallon; 12 to 16 servings

You might have heard it through the grapevine—for the coolest party refresher, this is one to serve!

½ gallon white grape juice, divided
2 liters ginger ale, divided

½ cup seedless green grapes
1 lemon, thinly sliced

In a 2-cup mold or small bowl, combine 1 cup grape juice and 1 cup ginger ale; mix well. Cover and freeze for at least 8 hours, or until firm. Meanwhile, chill the remaining grape juice and ginger ale. When ready to serve, unmold the frozen mixture and place in a punch bowl. Add the chilled grape juice and ginger ale, the grapes, and lemon slices; mix well and serve.

Note: If you'd like, add some additional grapes and lemon slices to the mold and freeze them with the grape juice and ginger ale.

Lemon-Lime Sherbet Punch

about 5 quarts; 16 to 20 servings

If you're lucky enough to be invited to a Southern wedding or rehearsal party, chances are you'll be toasting the happy couple with this!

4 cups cold water
3 cups pineapple juice, chilled
1 cup sugar
⅔ cup sweetened lemonade mix

1 quart lime sherbet, softened
2 liters ginger ale, chilled

In a punch bowl, combine the water, pineapple juice, sugar, and lemonade mix, stirring until the sugar and lemonade mix have dissolved. Using an ice cream scoop, add individual scoops of the sherbet to the punch bowl. Add the ginger ale, mix well, and serve.

Note: If you prefer, the lime sherbet can be left as a block or frozen in a ring mold and added to the punch that way.

Lemony Cola Punch

Serve this cola cooler sparked with a hint of lemon when you really want a drink that'll hit the spot!

3 cups cold water
¼ cup lemon juice
1 cup sugar

2 cans (12 ounces each) cola, chilled
Ice cubes

In a large pitcher, combine the water, lemon juice, and sugar, stirring until the sugar has dissolved. Add the cola; mix well. Serve in individual glasses over ice.

Note: When making this for a punch bowl, double the quantity of all the ingredients.

Coffee and Cream Punch

about 2½ quarts; 8 to 10 servings

Like a giant ice cream float, this one will draw kids young and old!

½ cup hot water
1 teaspoon vanilla extract
3 tablespoons instant coffee
  granules
3½ cups cold water

1 quart vanilla ice cream,
  softened
1 pint chocolate ice cream,
  softened
1 cup heavy cream

In a punch bowl, combine the hot water, vanilla, and coffee granules, stirring until the granules are completely dissolved. Add the cold water; mix well. Drop the vanilla and chocolate ice cream by ice cream scoopfuls into the coffee mixture. Using a spoon, swirl the heavy cream into the punch. Serve immediately.

Wedding Punch

about 2 quarts; 6 to 8 servings

Drink to the newlyweds' happiness with this wedding favorite. Since it's a bubbly refresher, I guess you could say it's perfect when served up with a toast!

2 cans (6 ounces each)
    pineapple juice, chilled
1 cup cold water
¼ cup lemon juice
½ cup sugar

1 package (4-serving size)
    lime-flavored gelatin
1 liter ginger ale, chilled
Ice cubes

In a large pitcher, combine the pineapple juice, water, lemon juice, sugar, and gelatin mix, stirring until the sugar and gelatin have dissolved. Add the ginger ale; mix well. Serve in individual glasses over ice.

Note: For a punch bowl, double the quantity of all the ingredients. If you want a totally sparkling wedding punch, replace the water with club soda.

Planter's Rum Punch

about 1 quart; 6 to 8 servings

Rum certainly is a popular choice in Southern kitchens, and when it's teamed with fruit juice, you get a drink that's suitable for almost anyone . . . anyone of age, that is.

3 cups pineapple juice
1 cup orange juice
¼ cup fresh lime juice

½ cup dark Jamaican rum
Crushed ice

In a large pitcher, combine all the ingredients except the ice, stirring to mix well. Serve in individual glasses over crushed ice.

Note: This will traditionally serve 6 to 8 . . . or 1 very romantic couple who's not driving anywhere!

Kentucky Eggnog

about 2 quarts; 6 to 8 servings

Spiked or plain, this Kentucky favorite is a year-round pleaser.

4 cups (1 quart) heavy cream,
  well chilled, divided
1 cup egg substitute
  (see Note)

¾ cup sugar
2 cups milk
½ cup bourbon (optional)
¼ teaspoon ground nutmeg

In a large bowl, whip 1 cup heavy cream with an electric beater on medium speed until stiff peaks form. In a punch bowl, combine the egg substitute and sugar, stirring until the sugar has dissolved. Add the remaining 3 cups heavy cream, the whipped cream, milk, bourbon, if desired, and the nutmeg. Whisk until well blended and serve immediately.

Note: You're asking why I use egg substitute instead of fresh eggs? Because I'd rather not serve anything made with raw eggs. Although this is good for all ages when you make it without the bourbon, be sure to keep it an adults'-only drink when you make it with bourbon.

Syllabub

about 1 quart; 4 to 6 servings

That's a great name, isn't it? If you drink this till the cows come home, oh, you'll be smiling while you wait.

1 cup (½ pint) heavy cream,
   well chilled
1 cup cold milk

1 tablespoon sugar
2 tablespoons whiskey

In a large bowl, beat the heavy cream, milk, and sugar with an electric beater on high speed until the mixture is foamy. Add the whiskey and beat for 1 to 2 minutes, or until the mixture is foamy again. Spoon into individual glasses and serve immediately.

Note: Make sure to beat this only until foamy; if you overbeat it, you'll end up with whipped cream! And if you'd like it sweeter, add another tablespoon or two of sugar.

DON'T OVERBEAT ME OR I'LL TURN TO BUTTER!

MILK

CREAM

Mint Julep

1 serving

Don't let the name mint julep fool ya'. It kind of sounds like a big mint milkshake, but it's far from that—it's bourbon with a touch of sugar and plenty of fresh mint. This refreshing drink is popular at the Kentucky Derby and throughout most of the South, and boy, it really packs a punch!

10 fresh mint leaves, plus
   1 whole sprig for garnish
1 tablespoon confectioners'
   sugar

¼ cup bourbon
Ice cubes

In a cocktail shaker or large glass, combine the mint leaves and the confectioners' sugar. Using the back of a spoon, crush the mint for 1 to 2 minutes, dissolving the sugar. Add the bourbon and stir until well blended. Pour into a 6-ounce glass filled with ice and garnish with a sprig of mint. Serve immediately.

Note: For more than 1 serving, just multiply the quantity of ingredients times the number of servings you need and prepare the recipe in a large pitcher. This drink is absolutely for adults only. And all of us adults need to remember this: **Never drink and drive!**

Index

ambrosia, 301
angel flake biscuits, 5
apple:
    -cinnamon finger
      sandwiches, 107
    coffee cake, 275
    -cranberry casserole, 229
    -raisin glazed ham, 152
    warm rings, 230
apricot-yam chicken bake, 170
Asian-marinated pork chops, 147
asparagus casserole, 201

bacon-honey barbecue sauce,
    126
banana:
    pudding parfait, 299
    punch, sparkling, 326
barbecue, 109–128
barbecue sauces:
    on basting with, 109
    bourbon, 128
    honey-bacon, 126
    lemon marinade, 125
    lip-smackin', 127
    North Carolina, 124
    sweet, 122
bean(s):
    butter, and ham soup, 42
    green, Southern casserole,
      213
    home-baked, 202
    steamin' taters 'n', 214
    three-, salad, 71
beef(y):
    barbecued short ribs, 114

bourbon steaks, 136
chicken bake, pleasin', 171
cola roast, 132
country-fried steak, 131
down-home meat loaf, 139
family reunion brisket, 138
Fourth of July hash, 50
golden roll-ups, 92
hamburger meal in one, 142
liver and onions, 144
old-fashioned pot roast, 135
peanut flank steak, 112
roll, ground, 143
salt-crusted, 133
sauerbraten with gingersnap
    gravy, 137
Southern stew, 55
Southern-style brisket, 113
stew, creamy oven-baked, 52
stovetop barbecued roast,
    111
Stroganoff, 134
stuffed cabbage bundles,
    140–141
beer rolls, 8
beet(s):
    easy pickled, 22
    salad, chilled, 82
    un-beet-able cake, 274
beverages, 319–335
biscuits:
    angel flake, 5
    buttermilk, 3
    cheese, 6
    soda, 4
bisque, tomato-crab, 48
blackened catfish, 184

black-eyed peas, 203
  hoppin' John, 246
blueberry golden crumb
  cobbler, 287
bourbon:
  barbecue sauce, 128
  fruitcake, 271
  steaks, 136
bread custard pudding, 298
breads, 1–18
Brie-oyster soup, 45
brisket:
  family reunion, 138
  Southern-style, 113
broccoli:
  snappy bake, 247
  summer's best salad, 69
brownie bars, marbled, 312
Brunswick stew, 51
butter(y):
  glazed carrots, 206
  mints, 316
  pecan fudge, 313
  potato balls, 238
  sticky roll-ups, 310
  vanilla frosting, 278
buttermilk:
  biscuits, 3
  chicken, tangy, 172
  -topped spuds, 237

cabbage:
  creamed, 204
  fried, 205
  stuffed bundles, 140–141
cakes, 251–278
canapés, peach, 106
caramel-nut cake, 270
carrot(s):
  butter-glazed, 206
  -pineapple salad, 78
catfish:
  blackened, 184

  fingers, purr-fect, 187
  fried, 181
cauliflower, cheesy, 207
cheese, cheesy:
  biscuits, 6
  cauliflower, 207
  Cheddar potato casserole,
   235
  chicken, baked, 176
  chicken bundles, 174–175
  crisps, 94
  crunchy macaroni and, 250
  eggplant-squash bake, 212
  flounder, baked, 182
  ham baked in crust of, 154
  ham roll-ups, 88
  nutty crackers, 97
  pimiento ball, 86
  pimiento sandwiches, 104
  pineapple, baked, 232
  -potato soup, 44
  straws, 91
cherry-cola salad, 79
cherry-nut holiday logs, 307
chess pie, lemon, 281
chicken:
  apricot-yam bake, 170
  bake, creamy, 163
  bake, pleasin' beefy, 171
  baked cheesy, 176
  barbecue chip, 120
  casserole, creamy, 173
  cheesy bundles, 174–175
  country rice and, 164
  'n' dumplings, shortcut, 167
  Fourth of July hash, 50
  hearty gumbo, 49
  mustard-pecan fillets, 168
  the one and only fried, 161
  peach-glazed, 119
  peachy glazed, 166
  with peanuts, 162
  pot pie casserole, 165
  salad, curried, 67

cheesy roll-ups, 88
country breakfast with red-
eye gravy, 156
glazed smoked picnic, 155
pie, hearty, 153
skillet glazed, 151
hamburger meal in one, 142
hash, Fourth of July, 50
hoecakes, plantation, 16
holiday cherry-nut logs, 307
hominy sausage casserole, 148
honey-bacon barbecue sauce,
126
hoppin' John, 246
hot dogs with chili sauce, 145
hush puppies, 242

iced tea, simply refreshing, 325
Irish potato soup, 41

jelly, pepper, 38
tarts, 95
Jerusalem artichokes, pickled, 24
julep, mint, 335

Kentucky eggnog, 333

lamb, glazed leg of, 157
lane cake, 264–265
lemon:
barbecue marinade, 125
chess pie, 281
cola punch, 329
country lemonade, 321
-lime sherbet punch, 328
sunny pie, 288
lime-pineapple mold, nutty, 76
liver and onions, 144
logs, holiday cherry-nut, 307
lower-fat cooking, xvii–xix

macaroni:
and cheese, crunchy, 250
Yankee Doodle casserole, 248
mandarin orange salad, 81
mango chutney spread, 85
marinade:
on basting with, 109
lemon barbecue, 125
marmalade, peach, 37
mayo rolls, easy, 9
meatballs, cola, 89
meat loaf, down-home, 139
meats, 129–158
mint julep, 335
mints, butter, 316
muffins:
molasses, 11
peanut butter, 12
mushroom(s):
Carolina marinated, 27
rice bake, 245
mustard:
-pecan chicken fillets, 168
sweet, barbecued chicken,
121
-wine Cornish hens, 178

nut(ty):
caramel cake, 270
cheese crackers, 97
cherry holiday logs, 307
pineapple-lime mold, 76
see also peanut; pecan

okra:
boiled, 216
fried, 215
pickled, 25
olive and egg sandwich strips,
105
onion-cracker pie, 217
onions, liver and, 144

Mr. Food® Can Help You Be A Kitchen Hero!

Let **Mr. Food**® make your life easier with Quick, No-Fuss Recipes and Helpful Kitchen Tips for

Family Dinners • Soups and Salads • Potluck Dishes • Barbecues • Special Brunches • Unbelievable Desserts

. . . and that's just the beginning!

Complete your **Mr. Food**® cookbook library today. It's so simple to share in all the *"OOH IT'S SO GOOD!!®"*

✂ -

TITLE	PRICE	QUANTITY	
A. **Mr. Food**® Cooks Like Mama	@ $12.95 each	x _____	= $_____
B. The **Mr. Food**® Cookbook, *OOH IT'S SO GOOD!!*®	@ $12.95 each	x _____	= $_____
C. **Mr. Food**® Cooks Chicken	@ $ 9.95 each	x _____	= $_____
D. **Mr. Food**® Cooks Pasta	@ $ 9.95 each	x _____	= $_____
E. **Mr. Food**® Makes Dessert	@ $ 9.95 each	x _____	= $_____
F. **Mr. Food**® Cooks Real American	@ $14.95 each	x _____	= $_____
G. **Mr. Food**®'s Favorite Cookies	@ $11.95 each	x _____	= $_____
H. **Mr. Food**®'s Quick and Easy Side Dishes	@ $11.95 each	x _____	= $_____
I. **Mr. Food**® Grills It All in a Snap	@ $11.95 each	x _____	= $_____
J. **Mr. Food**®'s Fun Kitchen Tips and Shortcuts (and Recipes, Too!)	@ $11.95 each	x _____	= $_____
K. **Mr. Food**®'s Old World Cooking Made Easy	@ $14.95 each	x _____	= $_____
L. "Help, **Mr. Food**®! Company's Coming!"	@ $14.95 each	x _____	= $_____
M. **Mr. Food**® Pizza 1-2-3	@ $12.00 each	x _____	= $_____
N. **Mr. Food**® Meat Around the Table	@ $12.00 each	x _____	= $_____
O. **Mr. Food**® Simply Chocolate	@ $12.00 each	x _____	= $_____
P. **Mr. Food**® A Little Lighter	@ $14.95 each	x _____	= $_____
Q. **Mr. Food**® From My Kitchen to Yours: Stories and Recipes from Home	@ $14.95 each	x _____	= $_____
R. **Mr. Food**® Easy Tex-Mex	@ $11.95 each	x _____	= $_____
S. **Mr. Food**® One Pot, One Meal	@ $11.95 each	x _____	= $_____
T. **Mr. Food**® Cool Cravings: Easy Chilled and Frozen Desserts	@ $11.95 each	x _____	= $_____
U. **Mr. Food**®'s Italian Kitchen	@ $14.95 each	x _____	= $_____
V. **Mr. Food**®'s Simple Southern Favorites	@ $14.95 each	x _____	= $_____

Book Total $_____

+ Postage & Handling for *First Copy* $ **4.00**

+ $1 Postage & Handling for Ea. Add'l. Copy
(Canadian Orders Add Add'l. $2.00 *Per Copy*) $_____

Send payment to:
Mr. Food®
P.O. Box 9227
Coral Springs, FL 33075-9227

Subtotal $_____

Name _____

Street _____ Apt._____

Add 6% Sales Tax
(FL Residents Only) $_____

City _____ State_____ Zip_____

BKV1

Total in U.S. Funds $_____

Method of Payment: ☐ Check or ☐ Money Order Enclosed

Please allow up to 6 weeks for delivery.